CONTENTS

CW00400370

DARREN BRIDGER

DECODING THE IRRATIONAL CONSUMER

How to commission, run and generate insights from neuromarketing research

MARKETING SCIENCE SERIES

KoganPage

LONDON PHILADELPHIA NEW DELHI

First published in Great Britain and the United States in 2015 by Kogan Page Limited

2nd Floor, 45 Gee Street	1518 Walnut Street, Suite 1100	4737/23 Ansari Road
London EC1V 3RS	Philadelphia PA 19102	Daryaganj
United Kingdom	USA	New Delhi 110002
www.koganpage.com		India

© Darren Bridger, 2015

The right of Darren Bridger to be identified as the author of this work has been asserted by him in accordance with the Copyright, Designs and Patents Act 1988.

ISBN   978 0 7494 7384 6
E-ISBN   978 0 7494 7385 3

British Library Cataloguing-in-Publication Data

A CIP record for this book is available from the British Library.

Library of Congress Cataloging-in-Publication Data

Bridger, Darren.
   Decoding the irrational consumer : how to commission, run and generate insights from neuromarketing research / Darren Bridger.
      pages cm. – (Marketing science)
      ISBN 978-0-7494-7384-6 (paperback) – ISBN 978-0-7494-7385-3 (ebk)   1. Marketing research.
2. Consumer behavior.   I. Title.
   HF5415.2.B676 2015
   658.8'34–dc23

                                                                                            2015022723

Typeset by Graphicraft Limited, Hong Kong
Print production managed by Jellyfish
Printed and bound by CPI Group (UK) Ltd, Croydon, CR0 4YY

For my parents

FOREWORD

Why are you reading this book? What made you choose it from the selection of books with a similar content, topic and even jacket? Do you really know? Was it the way in which the cover stood out relative to the context on the shelf or the web page? Was it the way in which the title leads to an emotional bump? Was it the colours or the imagery?

In tracing back to your decision-making process that eventually made you come to this situation – the book in your hand and reading these words – you probably realize that the decision was not made at one crucial step. If you didn't notice the book, you wouldn't have been able to have an emotional response to it. If you didn't have an emotional response, it's very likely that you would not have spent more time on the book. Exploring the book is a decision itself that relies on these steps, and the purchasing decision is only the most overt and sentient part of this process.

Purchasing products and services is a major part of our modern everyday lives. Even the choice *not* to buy something is a purchasing behaviour. Not surprisingly, there is a major interest in understanding the process of buying. What makes consumers interested? How can consumers' attention be guided to products and vital information?

For a long time, it was believed that consumers' choices were the result of a tedious and linear process: first we saw something and paid attention to it; we then gathered information about the product (price, relative value, need) and we ended up summing up these pros and cons to make up our minds to purchase the product or not. Following this line of reasoning, if we needed to understand consumers, all we needed to do was to ask them. Surveys and interviews served as valid and reliable ways to understand the consumer decision-making process.

Soon, however, we realized that consumer choices had other drivers. Advances in psychology showed us that non-conscious processes could be drivers of choice and behaviour, processes that we as consumers are neither privy to nor able to communicate to outsiders. At best, these processes manifest as gut feelings and hunches that a decision 'feels right' or 'feels wrong'. But in reality, the true drivers of consumption behaviours are hidden. Consumers are not linear, conscious or fully informed agents.

When Brian Knutson at Stanford University asked participants to watch and buy products while being brain scanned, he made a remarkable discovery. When his participants first saw products for four seconds, then saw a price for four seconds, and ultimately chose to buy or not buy the product within four seconds, all participants reported that their decision was made during those last four seconds. But when looking at brain responses during the first four seconds – when participants were only looking at the products – Knutson found that brain activity was highly predictive of their subsequent choice. That is, 8–12 seconds prior to consciously making up their minds, their brains had already made up their minds! A small structure called the nucleus accumbens was the driver of this unconscious motivation. Hidden from conscious access, this structure has a strong hold on the brain's wanting motivation, and stronger responses in this region signal an increased motivation to pursue, attend, learn and ultimately choose whatever triggers this response.

In the past decade or so, we have seen an exponential increase in academic papers demonstrating many non-conscious drivers of consumption behaviours. Leading academic journals in the neurosciences, psychology and economics bring novel findings that expand our understanding of our own behaviour as consumers. In the same period, industry has caught on, trying to build upon these insights, in creating new commercial fields such as neuromarketing. Today, no major international company tries to understand consumer behaviour without including some understanding of the non-conscious, intuitive consumer.

The ongoing exponential growth in technology and innovation constantly provides novel solutions to assess consumers. Eye-tracking, brain scanning and facial coding do not only operate as offline solutions in lab environments. Online solutions for assessing visual attention and emotional expressions are used at an increasing rate; computational models predict visual attention and cognitive workload; recent advances in brain scanning allow testing in mobile environments ranging from amusement parks to interaction with robots.

But with this abundance of research methods also comes confusion. Today, the industry is overwhelmed by the sheer number of solutions available, and only the fewest of practitioners and professionals will be able to tell apart the pros and cons of different methods.

There is a need for clarity in this vast clutter. And this is why you should read this book. We need to better understand the tools that are available, what their added values are and their limitations, but also how we can understand consumer behaviours. What better way than to have this book guide you through the different methods and insights? You'll enjoy it. My gut tells me.

Thomas Z Ramsøy, PhD
Founder and CEO of Neurons Inc,
Director, Center for Decision Neuroscience,
Copenhagen Business School and author of
Introduction to Neuromarketing & Consumer Neuroscience

PREFACE

This is a book about a new industry, barely a decade old, which has largely developed unseen by the outside world. Since the mid-2000s a new type of marketing and advertising research facility has spread around the globe. Usually in innocuous locations, in suburban office parks or corporate headquarters, these 'neuro-labs' on the surface resemble smart relaxed clinics, not dissimilar perhaps to your local dentist's. Invited members of the public will be seen arriving at these locations, where they fill in some paperwork and then sit in front of a large TV screen, as though at home. Yet they may next have sensors placed on their fingers, bodies or heads, or be positioned in front of an eye-tracking camera. Generally they are asked few or no questions, but the signals emanating from their bodies and brains will be carefully captured. Their reactions to what they see on the screen will subsequently be used to inform decisions about what we all see in TV ads, pick off the shelves in the supermarket, and even the designs of the products we use. The chances are overwhelming that every week the ads that you see or the products you place in your kitchen cupboards have been influenced by the findings from these studies.

For the last 15 years I have helped set up many such facilities and research projects around the world. Whether it is devising studies to test movie posters or car designs in Europe, shopper behaviours in the United States, TV ads in the Middle East, electronic products in Asia, or package designs in Africa and Russia, I have seen the industry grow rapidly to encompass all regions and all sectors. Lately I have seen the industry diversify outside the specialist labs, with the use of both small portable sensors and online at-home testing, where new methods are used to measure the reactions of volunteers to ads and images on their own computers.

So far there have been few general overviews of all the main measures that the industry uses. This has partially been because many of the companies involved have been bound by commercial confidentiality and their natural desire to protect their intellectual property. It is also because many of the early companies specialized in only one or two of the range of measures, and hence would provide only a limited glimpse of the full toolbox. Neuromarketing is an interdisciplinary practice that combines knowledge from a range of fields. Some of the main ones are shown in

FIGURE 0.1   The fields of knowledge that contribute to neuromarketing

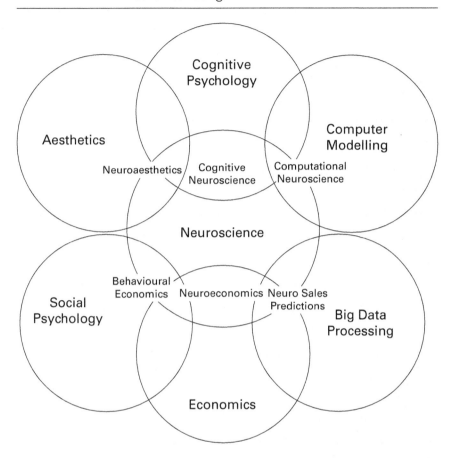

Figure 0.1. I wanted to write a book that helped open the toolbox a little more, and introduce people to each tool within, the ideas that make it work, and what can be done with it. I hope this book will be of particular interest to those working in marketing research who want an overview of neuromarketing, either to make decisions about commissioning such research, or just to feel more confident in understanding how the various techniques and theories contribute to it. It may also be of interest if you work in other areas of the marketing industry, particularly to the creatives who might want to understand more about the science and ideas that are increasingly being applied to marketing communications.

Darren Bridger
@DarrenLBridger

ACKNOWLEDGEMENTS

Kogan Page and the author gratefully acknowledge the involvement of Paul Conner, Philip Graves and Dr Raymond Bond, and thank them for providing valuable reviews of the manuscript for this book.

Author's acknowledgements

In writing this book I have drawn on the work of a wide array of researchers across different disciplines. In particular I would like to thank the following people for helping me in answering my questions and providing feedback: Pippa Bailey, Thomas Bayne, Paul Barrow, Richard Burton, Tammy Everts, Russell Fazio, Mike Follet, Eamon Fulcher, Joe Leech, Dan Machen, Bill Moult, Felix Morgan, Gawain Morrison, Martin De Munnik, Carla Negal, Thomas Ramsoy, Aaron Reed, Laurie Rudman, Kate Rutter, Richard Silberstein, Gareth Tuck, Ian Walsch and Steve Williams.

Special thanks to Thom Noble, Adam Field, Steve Genco, Paul Bretherton and the team at Kogan Page: Jasmin Naim, Jenny Volich and Megan Mondi, and editor Amanda Dackombe.

PART ONE
THEORETICAL INSIGHTS

THE IRRATIONAL CONSUMER: INTRODUCTION

01

In September 1772 Benjamin Franklin, one of the founding fathers of the United States and a key figure of the scientific Enlightenment, responded to a plea for help from a friend back in England. The chemist Joseph Priestley had been offered a job but was agonizing over whether to accept it. In Franklin's letter, he revealed his own method for making decisions. What he suggested was a kind of rational 'weighing up' that has become known as listing pros and cons. On a piece of paper, Franklin advised, one should create two parallel lists: one marked pro, one con. Then over the course of several days one should list each benefit and cost of a decision, and attempt to assign a number or weight to the importance of each. Finally, one can tally the weights of the pros versus those of the cons and arrive at the solution. It is almost an economist's dream: reducing the complexity and drama of human decision-making to a branch of arithmetic.

As economics and marketing developed, and people began to ask seriously how consumers decided what to buy, it was perhaps not surprising that the default assumption was that they performed some version of Franklin's pros versus cons calculation in their head; that they would at least weigh up, rationally, what was in their best interest and act accordingly. This view prevailed for many years until enough evidence accumulated that it was wrong. Whilst it may be an admirable ideal, consumers rarely engage in purely rational calculations. For most daily decisions it is far too time-consuming and tiring for us to perform exhaustive rational analyses. In fact, a common-sense consideration of our own behaviour should show us that we don't do this. If we made all our purchase decisions completely rationally, we would rarely buy any unhealthy foods – and our weekly grocery shopping would probably take hours as we sought to cross-reference all the variables of price, ingredients, volume and so on for each item. Yet even aside from not having the time and energy to evaluate every purchase decision, there are many ways in which consumers cannot give accurate, rational accounts of their behaviour. For example:

- Our purchases are often swayed by emotions that are fleeting or of which we are only dimly aware.
- Most people cannot accurately describe or quantify the full range of meanings and associations that a brand has for them. Yet a rich network of such meanings *does* exist in their mind.
- People are often unable to accurately describe why they bought something.

Instead of being rational consumers we rely on a range of ingenious mental shortcuts of which we are rarely consciously aware. Understanding these apparently irrational shortcuts and discovering how they are at play in the marketplace are the subject of this book.

How the view of the rational consumer crumbled

During the dawn of the growth of mass media advertising in the 1950s and 1960s there was an early interest in using psychological theories to understand how it worked. However, whilst there was an awareness of the power of non-conscious thought processes, the knowledge at the time was more heavily influenced by the work of Sigmund Freud and psychoanalysis, or behaviourism (which denied that we could measure the subconscious at all, and instead focused on stimulus–response learning), which have both been superseded by new models built on decades of experimental testing. At the time there was a growing unease amongst the public that the advertising industry might be manipulating us through the use of subliminal messages. This paranoia largely centred on a study reported in the late 1950s by James Vicary in which he claimed to have flashed, at just a three-thousandth of a second, the phrases 'Drink Coca-Cola' and 'Hungry? Eat Popcorn' on a cinema screen during a movie. Despite these sneaky entreaties being too fleeting for the cinema-goers to consciously notice, he claimed that sales of Coca-Cola and popcorn increased substantially. Yet a replication of the experiment was unable to produce the same result and he later admitted that he had lied. Nevertheless, spurred on by Vance Packard's book *The Hidden Persuaders* (1957), the public were becoming deeply suspicious of the antics of the advertising industry.

Perhaps understandably, advertisers – to protect their public image if nothing else – backed away from models of subconscious influences to concentrate instead on theories that emphasized the notion that consumers make rational choices about their purchases. Yet, ironically, as we shall see later, effects not dissimilar to Vicary's subliminal messages have been found to work and this time there is real data to back them up. Since the mid-1990s, a number of factors have come together to bring back the non-conscious model to the world of advertising and market research.

First, during the last couple of decades we have learned more about the way that the brain works than during all of previous recorded history. Brain scanners have become more powerful, and brain scientists have accumulated masses of data on how our minds work. Building on all this work there is now a range of techniques that are cheaper and faster to use than the clinical-type brain scanners. The benefit of these newer techniques is that they are fast and cheap to use, comparable to the cost of a typical market research survey, bringing these methods within the grasp of the market research community. It is this range of techniques and the theoretical frameworks that complement and help explain them that are the focus of this book.

Second, there has been a growing awareness of the limitations of tools such as surveys and focus groups. Consumers are not always able to articulate why they have bought things in the past, and can find it even harder to imagine what they might want to buy in the future. For example, Henry Ford famously said, 'If I had asked people what they wanted, they'd have said a faster horse'; Akio Morita, the co-founder of Sony, said (in the context of the development of the Walkman), 'We don't ask consumers what they want. They don't know.' So if we want to uncover fresh insights into what is really driving consumers, then simply asking them might not be enough.

In order to understand why consumers can be irrational, we can study the signals given off by their bodies, the positions of their eyes, movements of facial expressions and the subtleties of their behaviour under carefully controlled conditions. Marrying this with new theories and findings from the brain science labs can give us a whole new perspective. The model or paradigm that the new findings imply is worlds away from the traditional view of the rational consumer that marketers had been labouring under. Table 1.1 shows some of the key differences.

However, in order to first understand why consumers can appear irrational, we need to return to our roots and take a brief look at how our brains evolved.

Hunter-gatherers in the shopping mall

The force that shaped the development of our brains was day-to-day survival in the East African savannahs over millennia, not abstract sophisticated thinking in urban high-tech environments of the 21st century. Staying alive was the impetus behind evolving a brain in the first place: seeking out food, and avoiding starvation or attack from predators. This meant that in terms of the brain's thinking, three things were paramount: threat detection, speed and energy efficiency.

TABLE 1.1   Comparing the old and new ways of viewing consumers

The Old Model	The New Model
Advertisers need to grab and hold consumers' conscious attention in order to deliver their messages.	Messages and emotions are routinely embedded in our memories without us paying high levels of conscious attention to them.
Consumers need to be rationally persuaded of the benefits of a product or service in order for it to be successful.	Consumers are just as likely to be driven by emotional cues and non-conscious heuristics as by rational persuasion.
Consumers more or less know what they want and can tell you if you ask them.	Consumers don't always know what they want and don't always know or have the ability to articulate their behaviour and reactions.
How much a consumer is willing to pay for a product is a direct function of its value to them.	Perceived value is often a subjective thing for consumers, and subject to non-conscious and irrational influences.

Our brains are rapaciously energy-hungry organs. Despite comprising just 2 per cent of our body weight, they use up to 25 per cent of its energy. Clearly, anything that the brain can do to use less power will be of advantage, as it would stop the person running out of energy and starving. Over time, our ancestors' brains evolved shortcuts to thinking that would save energy. As nothing seems to give our brains the glucose-munchies like conscious, rational, deliberative thinking, we needed an 'energy saving' mode of thought. Equally, in situations of possible threat, if our hunter-gatherer ancestors had taken the time to consciously, rationally weigh up the chances that the movement they saw in the corner of their eye was a lion, they may not have survived for very long. To underscore the point: it typically takes up to half a second or more for our brains to digest incoming sensory information and present a meaningful experience to our conscious mind. This may seem fast, but its implications for avoiding predators could be fatal. Even today, our consciousness is constantly half a second behind reality, meaning that most activities – from sport to walking and even talking – are largely taken care of by our non-conscious minds (although the brain creates the bizarre illusion that our consciousness is in complete control!). Therefore, for millions of years Mother Nature has sculpted our brains with a preference for fast shortcut thinking.

Another reason why we weren't born to be fully rational is that our thinking is biased towards our own personal experience. We didn't evolve with access to finding out the experiences of others through books, mass media or scientific experiments. In general, if we hadn't seen or experienced it first hand, we didn't know about it. Therefore, most of our choices are disproportionately influenced by things we have personally experienced and we find it particularly difficult to think statistically. For example, rather than rational estimates of statistical likelihood, our thinking about probability is heavily influenced by the ease with which things come to mind.

It is the existence of these shortcuts and limitations that can often make consumer behaviour seem difficult to explain. The world we live in today is both highly complex and often quite unlike the East African savannahs in which our ancestors spent most of our evolutionary history. Take money, for example: whilst human societies have had some form of money for thousands of years, it is a relatively recent phenomenon in evolutionary terms. In contrast, what our brains actually evolved to make material value decisions about was food.

The ideas in this book do not require a detailed understanding of neuro anatomy but instead focus on the characteristics of two types of thinking done by our brains: conscious and non-conscious thinking. The high-speed, low-energy non-conscious form of thought is responsible for most of our cognition. So what is this mysterious *éminence grise* that directs so much of our behaviour?

The irrational non-conscious

At the birth of academic psychology in the late 19th century there was a growing awareness of the fact that much of what our brains do is veiled from our consciousness. This notion eventually gained public prominence in the ideas of Freud. Whereas Freud's model of the subconscious was a seething mass of repressed, primitive passions and childhood neuroses, our current model of the non-conscious is quite different. Instead it is more like a workhorse, taking care of most of our routine thinking, yet limited in its rationality. We now know that it is active all the time, not just responsible for keeping a lid on painful emotions. To distinguish this new model from Freud's subconscious, this book will refer to it as the non-conscious mind or 'system 1' thinking, with system 2 representing our conscious thought – terms coined by psychologists Keith Stanovich and Richard West. System 1, or the non-conscious, is always working away to make sense of our current environment, scanning it for the presence of threats or opportunities. Its thinking is 'quick and dirty', using the simplest routes – in an energy-efficient manner – to assess what is around us. However, system 1's frugal ways come at a cost. It is bad at thinking logically or statistically and is unaware of its own shortcomings. It automatically always proffers an opinion on everything, whether or not it has had enough information to properly do so. It gathers up all the information it has at hand and performs quick, rough assessments of it. For example, when we meet a new person or see a new product for the first time, we tend to instantly have a gut feeling about it – we rarely feel neutral and await more information before casting judgement, as a more rational mind might. To make a bad situation worse, rather than stress-test snap judgements by seeking ways in which they can be disproved (again, as a rational mind would), system 1 tends to prefer to seek information that confirms its beliefs. Finally, as though to add insult to injury, it is guilty of what psychologists call a 'halo effect': if it finds one good thing to form the basis of a good judgement, it will generalize that across all traits, and vice versa with a bad judgement.

Luckily, help is at hand in the form of system 2: our conscious, rational thinking. When things get too difficult for system 1 or it becomes aware of a looming threat, it will pass over responsibility to system 2. System 2 thinking is generally slower and requires more energy (depleting our blood glucose levels) – and this feels slightly unpleasant and effortful. It also eats up our attention, which is a finite resource. If we are focusing hard on system 2 thinking, we often become blind to other things going on around us. Nevertheless, it can think rationally, using logic, statistics and careful comparisons of multiple sources of information. However, even system 2 can sometimes be victim to irrationality as it is fed information and intuitions from system 1, which are often flawed.

TABLE 1.2   Features of system 1 and system 2 thinking

Consumers' Non-conscious (or System 1) Mode of Thought	Consumers' Conscious (or System 2) Mode of Thought
Always on	More active at some times than at other times
Fast and easy	Slower and more effortful
Uses emotions, memories and pattern recognition to make fast judgements and decisions	Is able to think more systematically, rationally and statistically in making judgements and decisions
Always proffers a judgement or feeling about a brand, service or product	Can recognize the importance of reserving judgement until more information is gathered
Is often unable to express itself in language; is outside conscious awareness	Creates verbal rationalizations for the choices of the non-conscious

Both systems are working continuously throughout our working day, passing tasks back and forth, albeit with the lazy system 2 usually happy to delegate nearly everything to system 1. After all, the effort of rational thought is somewhat unpleasant so it is only triggered when absolutely necessary. Whilst issues such as brand meanings, the nuances of pack designs and advertising campaigns can become the subject of marketers' obsessive attention, they are rarely deemed important enough by consumers to trigger their rational system 2 into action (see Table 1.2).

When we have to learn something new, such as how to use a new phone or how to drive a new car, system 2 predominates but then gradually we can pay less attention as system 1 takes over and the task becomes habitual. Much of the operations of system 1 are locked away from our conscious awareness and we cannot sense them even if we want to. Yet, strangely, we don't even have any sense that we are unable to consciously inspect these thought processes, which leaves us open to confabulating when asked about behaviour that is motivated by system 1.

For example, psychologists set up a test in a supermarket in Sweden asking shoppers to sample two different types of jam and say which they preferred. Once their preference had been noted, they were offered a second taste of their preferred jam and again asked to rate it, as well as to explain why they preferred it. However, unbeknown to the shoppers, each jam container was double-ended, containing the opposite jam at either end. In-between their first and second sample, one of the experimenters surreptitiously turned the jar so that on the second sample of their favourite jam the shoppers actually tasted the one they said they didn't like. Amazingly, only one in three ever realized the switch. However, not only did the majority not detect a difference, but they were also able to justify why they liked a jam that they actually didn't! The researchers found similar effects with choosing tea, and even choosing between which of two men or women were the more attractive in photographs![1]

This phenomenon – consumers not knowing why they really chose a product – is known as 'choice blindness'. At its worst it can lead our system 2 minds into concocting all manner of inventive tales in order to rationalize our purchases. Of course, a highly intuitive and skilled market researcher or focus-group leader may be able to see through these false explanations, or they may not. It is almost impossible to control. Our brains would probably have continued to get away with it if the experimental psychologists hadn't caught them in flagrante!

Nevertheless, our conscious minds must be given some slack. The average trip to a shopping mall or supermarket bombards our senses with so many stimuli and options that our conscious mind cannot possibly process it all rationally. It has been estimated that whilst our senses take in around 11 million bits per second our conscious minds can only process 50 bits per second. Clearly there is a vast amount of filtering taking place.

Irrational doesn't mean stupid

Whilst many cultures often prize rationality, to describe consumer behaviour as irrational is not to denigrate it or claim that it is necessarily unintelligent. Our non-conscious minds are highly sophisticated systems, having evolved over countless millions of years. Not only are they usually miraculously efficient at handling our daily activities, but by doing so they free up our conscious minds to do what they do best: more considered learning and planning for the future. 'The more of the details of our daily life we can hand over to the custody of automation,' wrote the psychologist William James, 'the more our higher powers of mind will be set free for their own proper work.'[2]

Dual-process decisions

Whilst the measures described in this book mainly capture system 1, non-conscious responses, real consumer behaviour and verbal reports are a mixture of influences from both systems. Neuroscientists and cognitive psychologists are currently debating how to model such interactions of influences, and such models are usually termed 'dual-system' or 'dual-process'.

An example of how this might work is a consumer standing in a super-market aisle choosing between a range of product options. Their system 1 thinking may provide a preference in terms of an intuitive feeling towards one option. If this preference feels strong then the person's system 2 thinking may accept it, perhaps providing a rationale for why they chose it. However, if system 1 provides a weak or incoherent preference then the shopper will begin to rely more heavily on system 2, and put more effort into thinking through which option to select.[3] Yet even in instances where system 2 is dominating a decision-making process, it is still likely to be pulling in system 1-type inputs, as the effect of past choices, the environment, the way that the choices are presented and visual cues on the packaging may all feed in at a non-conscious level. Also, even more system 2-dominated choices can be thought of as being boundedly rational (ie rational as possible within the practical limits of what a person knows – see more on this in Chapter 4), rather than purely rational. We rarely have all the information and time necessary to compute a fully rational decision, so our choices will be made from a limited range of information. Even in this situation, system 1 can still influence our thinking by helping us focus on which bits of information we consider to be meaningful to consider in making our choice.

Another example of when consumers might rely more on system 2 processes comes from the 'Elaboration Likelihood model'.[4] This argues that there are two routes to attitude formation: central and peripheral (analogous to system 2 and system 1, respectively). If a person is motivated and able to, then they will think more carefully and rationally about a claim that is put to them (such as an advertising or packaging claim about a product). If not, then the person is more likely to rely on environmental cues or mental biases to form their opinion.

The types of data that are hard to measure rationally

There are seven main areas in which traditional techniques (such as surveys and focus groups) can fall short in understanding the irrational consumer with traditional conscious self-report measures:

1 *Our ability to articulate emotional responses*
    Consumers do not always have the ability to articulate the array of emotions and feelings that an advert or product is evoking in them. This may be because they simply do not have the vocabulary, due to being unpractised at expressing their inner feelings, or just that these feelings are subtle and fleeting and therefore hard to pin down. For example, during the course of a 30-second advert or a 60-second interaction with a product, the consumer may go on a rapid emotional 'journey', during which they experience many feelings, perhaps at a low level, and unless they are particularly articulate and introspective then a typical survey question may fail to capture the richness of this experience.

2 *Cultural differences in expression*
    Even consumers who are able to articulate their emotions can do so differently from one another. How do you know which members of your sample may be exaggerating and which might be downplaying their responses? You may be able to capture which emotions are being activated but not to what degree. This challenge may be exacerbated when attempting cross-cultural studies. Not only can the vocabulary for emotional terms cover quite different territories between cultures, but different norms of expression can again distort the degree to which research participants are enthusiastic or dismissive in their responses.

3 *Social desirability bias*
    Whenever research is conducted face-to-face (either by a researcher or in the context of a focus group) there may be some opinions and reactions that consumers keep to themselves if they fear they may be judged adversely about them. Equally, there may be other opinions and reactions that they exaggerate or bring to the fore if they think it makes them look good. Of course, this is a

particular problem with socially sensitive subjects and it may be that your research questions are never that controversial. Yet there can be areas of questioning that may stray into areas in which people wish to display or hide their social status, fashionableness or intelligence. On more than one occasion I have seen a 'leader' emerge in a focus group whom the other participants subsequently – and presumably non-consciously – begin to 'mirror'. Usually the leader is someone particularly articulate, whose vocabulary the other participants latch on to and begin to repeat.

4 *Limits of memory*

Our conscious memory (usually called 'declarative memory' by psychologists: the memories that we are able to talk about) has limits. Most people do not pay much attention to routine behaviours such as shopping in the supermarket. Therefore, questions about how they have made decisions in the past may be hard to answer as they just can't remember. Also, in a similar way to point 1 above, emotional reactions can be so fleeting and can successively change from one moment to the next when viewing an ad or interacting with a product that it is almost impossible for most consumers to accurately recall them.

There are attempts to get around this problem. First, the researcher could replay the ad, and pause every so often or get the respondent to talk over it, describing their responses as it plays. However, they have then transformed the experience into something unnatural – most of us don't consciously inspect our feelings as we watch an ad, and simultaneously divide our attention between it and talking about it to a researcher. Even the act of hearing ourselves bringing our own reactions to light by talking about them may change our reactions! Second, researchers can use a dial or buttons to get respondents to give a simple, binary (eg positive/negative or interesting/non-interesting) ongoing moment-by-moment reaction to an ad. This may be a less problematic task for them than verbally describing their reactions, but it still suffers from the problem that asking people to introspect and divide their attention whilst watching something means that you are no longer getting a 'pure' reading of their responses.

5 *The difficulty in accurately quantifying responses*
There are times when you may want to chart responses on some form of numerical scale. For example, if you need to track responses over time, or to compare one group of respondents to another. However, using standard research techniques this can be difficult. Either you impose a coding system onto people's verbal responses, which may be imperfect, or you ask people to rate their own responses on some form of scale. Yet people are not necessarily that good at rating responses on a scale. There is often a tendency towards giving 'mediocre' responses near to the centre of the scale.

6 *The tendency to post-rationalize*
As many of our buying behaviours are driven by non-conscious and irrational decisions, there can be strong pressures to rationalize our choices when asked to explain them. Most people don't want to be seen as irrational, inconsistent or economically naive, therefore they will often invent a reason why they behaved the way they did. The situation becomes worse when you consider that we often cannot remember or just don't have conscious access to why we did something. Lastly, even though people have a tendency to post-rationalize, they may not even be aware that they are doing it, meaning that sorting out the real answers from the post-rationalized ones may just be an impossible task for the researcher.

7 *Some of our mental processes are hidden from introspection*
As many of our choices are processed non-consciously, they are hidden from our conscious introspection. As we have little awareness of the fact that there are non-conscious decisions being made in our brain all the time, when asked about why we did something, our conscious brain tends to prefer to make up an answer that makes sense to it than to admit it is not in complete control!

So if traditional techniques are often inadequate at decoding our irrational behaviour how can we uncover the forces that are driving consumers?

How the irrational can be decoded

This book presents two solutions to decoding the irrational consumer: first the theories that underpin why consumers are irrational. In order to begin to understand this behaviour it is helpful to take a multidisciplinary approach, drawing on neuroscience, psychology and anthropology as well as the new fields of behavioural economics, neuroeconomics and neuro-marketing. Each of these fields has useful insights that can help us study the consumers' non-conscious.

The second approach is in conducting consumer research. As consumers cannot always articulate what drives their desires or behaviours, we need to study their behaviour and the signals that their bodies and brains are giving off in order to infer what is driving them.

The two approaches can work beautifully in tandem: the theories help us design our research, and then interpret the findings. The ultimate aim is always to then gain new insights into how and why your consumers are responding in the way they do. With judicious and creative thought, we should not only be able to confirm some of the existing best practices in advertising, design, and product and service creation, but derive new ones. Everything from web-user interface, to designing products, experiences, sonics, advertising etc should be able to be improved through the insights available through non-conscious research. Just as we can improve the ergonomics of products through a proper understanding of the mechanics of the human body, an understanding of the mechanics of the human brain – perception, decision-making, memory and attention – should yield better understanding of how to effectively emotionally engage with consumers.

The new toolbox

Neuroaesthetics: insights from neuroscience on what we find beautiful, pleasurable or attractive and why.

Behavioural economics: studies how people make decisions about value. For example, how people weigh up the cost/benefits of different gambles, or how people make judgements about how much products should cost.

Implicit response measures: these are computer-based tests that can be run online. They exploit the principle that the more we have been primed to think of a concept, the faster we react to something that our non-conscious mind connects to that concept. Implicit response measures can hence map the non-conscious associative memory networks that consumers have.

Facial action coding: there are six facial expressions of emotions that appear to be common across cultures. Using sophisticated software, even a webcam video feed of a person's face can be analysed moment by moment for signs of each of these emotions whilst the person watches a video.

Biometrics: there are several bodily signals that can be measured – including heart rate and skin conductance – that are indicative of how someone is responding emotionally to an experience.

Eye-tracking: by co-ordinating a camera view of a person's eyes with presentation of an image or view on-screen, we can measure exactly where the person was looking, what order they looked at each part of the screen, and how long their eyes lingered on each element.

EEG (electroencephalography): measuring patterns of electrical brain activity with sensors placed on the head.

fMRI (functional magnetic resonance imaging): measuring which areas of a person's brain are active by measuring blood flow in the brain. This requires that the person lies within a special scanner.

SST (steady state topography): similar to EEG, a measure of electrical brain activity, but which sets up a 'marker' frequency in the person's brain using a flickering light. As exposure to stimuli then makes the brain work, there are deviations in this frequency that allow us to see how hard areas of the brain are working.

Prediction markets: on certain research questions there may be a lot of 'noise' in the responses of individuals, but when aggregated together the group response as a whole can be uncannily accurate.

How companies are using this data

The techniques covered in this book are already being used around the world on a daily basis by marketers and researchers. Every major industry sector is using them, including auto, fast-moving consumer goods (FMCG), drinks, consumer electronics, finance, and entertainment and media. 'I've seen many new research techniques pop up over the years,' says marketing industry veteran Thom Noble, 'but they usually turn out to be fads or repackaged versions of existing methods. The exciting thing about applying neuroscience to marketing is that it can give a genuinely fresh, original and sometimes surprisingly different view on old problems. This newer, science-led approach is not offering just another gizmo in the traditional researcher's toolkit, but an access ticket to a parallel "neuroverse" of perception and insight.'[5]

These methods are being used to study almost every area of marketing activity, including brands, advertising (including print, TV, audio and web), packaging, in-store activities, concepts – and products themselves. Many tests are what we often refer to as 'beauty contests': choosing the best of several possible alternatives of package/display designs or advertising executions. As well as everyday marketing questions, these methods are also being used for more strategic research and development (R&D) or developmental-type questions. For example, by understanding the aspects of a product design that are most important to consumers, companies can spend their R&D budgets more efficiently. Or, by testing advertising at conceptual stage, refinements can be made pre-production, thus saving money.

In recent years consumer trends have only increased the pressure on marketers to understand what drives apparently irrational, emotional and non-conscious consumer behaviour. Until around the mid-1990s, it was still relatively easy in developed countries to reach a mass audience with TV or print advertisements. Like a bowling ball hurled at an array of pins, a message was launched and had a relatively uncomplicated path to its market of consumers. However, with the proliferation of TV channels, video-on-demand and the internet it has become harder to reach big groups with one shot. Rather than a bowling alley the consumer marketplace is now more like a pinball machine, with a potential consumer's mind ricocheting in different directions as they are exposed to brand messages from a myriad of 'touch points'. Social media, online video, online customer reviews and a proliferation of online stores have joined traditional media and the in-store experience as sources of brand information. As well as a more competitive and multifaceted environment, these new channels evoke new research questions. For example, the hot questions right now are how we shift our attention between screens – from the TV to the smartphone/tablet – or how the various touchpoints each contribute to a brand. These new techniques are ideally positioned to help answer those questions.

Summary

- Consumers' irrational thinking comes from our energy-saving non-conscious mode of thought (sometimes called system 1 thinking, or the subconscious).

- Marketers need to understand the non-conscious thinking behind many consumer choices.

- Asking questions can be of limited value in understanding non-conscious thinking. This is why market researchers are increasingly adopting a new range of techniques for measuring non-conscious responses.

Notes

1 Hall, L, Johansson, P, Tärning, B, Sikström, S and Deutgen, T (2010) Magic at the marketplace: choice blindness for the taste of jam and the smell of tea, *Cognition*, **117** (1), pp 54–61.
2 James, W (1890) *Principles of Psychology*, vol. 2, Holt, New York.
3 Dhar, R and Gorlin, M (2013) A dual-system framework to understand preference construction processes in choice, *Journal of Consumer Psychology*, **23** (4), pp 528–42.
4 Petty, R and Cacioppo, J (2011) *Communication and Persuasion: Central and peripheral routes to attitude change*, Springer-Verlag, New York.
5 Personal communication with the author.

THE BRAIN: ATTENTION, MEMORY AND EMOTION

02

Millions of years of evolution have bequeathed us brains of astonishing intricacy. Astronomical numbers about the brain abound: it is composed of around 86 billion neurons, each with anywhere between 1,000 and 10,000 connections, and contains 100,000 miles of blood vessels. Information can flow through the brain at up to 268 miles per hour. Such complexity means that neuroscientists study the brain from a number of different perspectives: its neurochemistry; the structures of individual neurons; the neuroanatomy (or the larger structures of the brain); as a system of processes; or the mathematical and computational rules that underlie its processes. Of most relevance to this book is the approach of cognitive neuroscience: the marrying of findings from psychological experiments with data on people's brain and bodily responses.

Sometimes an over-reliance on information on neuroanatomy can mislead. For example, even neuroscientists have been found to rate neuroscience studies as being of higher value simply if the study contains a brain image than if it doesn't (even if the study without the brain image is otherwise more or less identical).[1] Nevertheless, basic familiarity with some broad features of neuroanatomy is useful in understanding the measures that we get from the techniques covered in this book.

There are obviously many categories of activities that our brains do, including planning, pursuing goals, and controlling our bodies and mouths to produce behaviour and speech. However, much of the research in neuromarketing relates to three core brain activities: attention, memory and emotion. Each one of these areas has a vast body of related research and literature on each. Obviously, therefore, there is not space here to cover everything. Instead, we'll focus on the areas that are of most relevance to marketing and advertising, and that are of greatest applicability in interpreting the findings of the types of non-conscious research covered in this book.

Attention

Understanding attention is of increasing importance in marketing as consumers' attention becomes an ever-scarcer resource. Compared to several decades ago, consumers may often be richer in purchasing-power terms, but are almost certainly poorer in attention. Myriad more entertainments, commercial messages and information of all kinds assail our senses throughout our waking days than ever before. Many brands now have a wider array of incarnations, or touch points, not to mention places that they can deliver their messages. Understanding the relative patterns of attention that consumers pay to each has become a pressing concern. Younger consumers in particular are usually more comfortable in this environment, switching their attention rapidly between sources such as the TV, their mobile phone, tablet or computer screen, whilst maybe listening to music at the same time! However, whilst some people are more comfortable with this type of multitasking, it usually comes at the price of less in-depth focus.

By looking at a few key facts about how attention works we can arrive at some useful and relevant guidelines.

Attention is both bottom-up and top-down

Probably most attention-related processing in our brains relates to our vision.

Essentially there is only a small region of our visual field that we are able to see in any detail, but our brains manage to hide this from our conscious awareness through moving our eyes almost continuously, and also using assumptions about the world to instantaneously stitch together a seamless tapestry of the visual landscape around us.

As information enters the brain from our optic nerves it gets routed in several directions. First there is low-level categorization of features such as areas of contrast that might denote the edges of objects, brightness, contrasts and colours. These features are all variable in appearance depending on the angle, distance, illumination levels etc. For example, a piece of coal in harsh bright sunlight can give off a brighter hue than a piece of white paper in the dark. Yet our brain's knowledge of the real colours of these two objects shapes our perception such that we still see the coal as dark black and the paper as clear white. That is because whilst our brains are decoding these low-level features, information is coming back down from higher brain regions that are already working to decode what the object is, guiding our perception. After the initial processing of the low-level features, our brain groups them together into shapes and objects. Finally, with input from 'higher' brain regions, meaning is assigned to what we are looking at.

The overall key point of all this is that seeing is an active process, constantly being informed by our memories, assumptions of what we are looking at and the environment around us. It is top-down as well as bottom-up. Context, expectation and memories all influence where we focus our attention, and how we perceive and interpret what we are seeing. 'Perception,' says psychologist Roger Shepard, 'is externally guided hallucination.'[2] Another implication, as we will see in Chapter 6 on eye-tracking, is that it may be important to make logos or package designs distinctive and easy to recognize from their low-level features, such as their unique colours, as these are the first things that we process.

Limits to attention

Everyone knows what attention is. It is the taking possession by the mind, in clear and vivid form, of one out of what seem several simultaneously possible objects or trains of thought. It implies withdrawal from some things in order to deal effectively with others.[3]

The above quote from 19th-century psychologist William James reminds us that our attention is a choice: we direct what we pay attention to, but that volitional focus is finite. Whilst we have only a relatively limited field of high focus, our non-conscious is constantly scanning the rest of the environment for areas of interest that we will then focus on. In vision, things that look promising and interesting in our peripheral field can be brought into our attention through moving our eyes to them. In sound, there is the cocktail-party effect, whereby even if you are engrossed in conversation with the person directly in front of you in a crowded room, and someone suddenly mentions your name across the room, you immediately notice. On some non-conscious level you were already aware of a wider array of conversations. Our field of non-conscious attention is constantly monitoring and processing far more than we know.

We are sometimes blind without knowing it

As every good magician knows, the eye directed towards one thing can easily miss another. In one of the more infamous published psychological studies of recent years, participants are asked to view a video clip of a small crowd of people rapidly passing basketballs between one another. Half are wearing white T-shirts, the other half are wearing black T-shirts. The task is to count the passes between the players wearing white tops. Whilst doing this, a significant number of people fail to notice a person in a gorilla suit walking past the camera. The experiment creates an attention 'sink' by combining movement with intense focus.[4] This is an example of a phenomenon known as 'inattentional blindness'.

Our eyes are directed towards movement (particularly in our peripheral vision; images that flicker at 2–4 HZ are also especially attention-grabbing), and attention can be artificially grabbed and held in ads that use fast and frequent editing cuts. Even the experience of a smooth visual world around us is somewhat an illusion constructed by our brains: the information received from our eyes is actually very jumpy as our eyes are making regular movements (called saccades), and as the eyes make each movement there is a brief moment of blindness (which keeps us unaware of the saccading) that our brains cover up. The relevance of these lapses in awareness is that if a key piece of information – such as branding – occurs at these moments, it can be completely missed. Hence the frequent phenomenon of people remembering an ad, but not remembering which brand it was for. There are several other key ways in which we regularly miss things:

- *Change blindness*: as we saw in Chapter 1 – with the example of people not noticing that two jams they had just tasted had been switched around before they had a second taste – we often miss the differences between things. The actual perceptual differences between products (eg their taste) may not always be the key factor in whether we like them. Context and expectations bias our experiences. This can be used by website and package designers: consumers often dislike abrupt changes to the design of things they use regularly (such as websites), but by changing them gradually over time the changes are less likely to be perceived and cause discomfort (websites such as Yahoo and eBay have used this tactic to make changes to the look of their sites).

- *Attentional blink*: this is an effect that comes into play when you have a succession of fast-cut images. If an image appears that is particularly attention-grabbing or attracts extra mental resources to decode (for example a surprising image) we are less likely to notice anything that appears within around half a second afterwards. The implications of this to marketing may seem limited to fast-cut ads, but it may also be worth considering giving enough space or time around information that you want people to consciously notice, so that it doesn't get overshadowed by adjacent information that might act as an attention 'sink'.

- *Event boundaries*: as our brains follow a flow of information, such as the storyline of an ad, they are constantly categorizing what is happening into discrete events.[5] Rather than storing a complete video-like memory of the ad, this process enables our brains to store it as a series of discrete 'snapshots'. However, information presented just after the end of one of these boundaries is likely to be forgotten. The end of an event could be marked by a change of scene, subject, or something like the punchline of a joke.

- *Habituation*: as we get used to repetitive sensory stimulation, it falls out of our awareness. For example, if you enter a room with a ticking clock, you may hear it at first, but after a while the sound seems to disappear as your brain habituates to it.

To summarize: our attention is fallible, and we regularly fail to consciously notice things. However, whilst we consciously miss a lot, we non-consciously absorb more than we realize.

We see more than we are consciously aware of

High attention levels have historically been held up to be the most important thing in retail and advertising. However, whilst understanding how attention works is very useful to marketers, generating lots of it may be of more relevance to communicating to our rational, conscious minds than our irrational non-conscious. For example, the media that probably benefit most from grabbing high levels of attention are communications online (where arresting attention may be crucial to avoid the person simply clicking away from the page, rather than playing your video or clicking on your banner), in-store displays (where if your product doesn't get noticed, it won't get picked up), and communications that involve short-term tactical information, such as special offers and deals. Also, communications that benefit from having consumers consciously and rationally think about your claims are better with high levels of attention. For example, if you need to communicate specific, unique or technical product features that you want people to be aware of (notwithstanding the old marketing dictum of selling the benefit rather than the feature!).

Attention and advertising

Whilst it is obviously important for your product to stand out at point of purchase (otherwise it might not be found), the benefits of high attention in advertising may have been overstated. Consider, for example, how often people avoid watching TV ads. When the ad break comes on many people see it as an opportunity to go to the bathroom, grab a drink, look down at their magazine/phone/tablet, speak to their family etc. Alternatively, they record shows and fast-forward through the ads (although some research has shown that TV ads viewed on fast-forward speed can, surprisingly, still be effective, particularly if brand information is displayed in the centre of the screen).[6] The situation is not helped by the fact that, according to surveys, a majority of people say they don't like advertising and they don't believe it persuades them. Perhaps, unsurprisingly, TV advertising doesn't work by directly consciously persuading us. After all, in the 1960s the psychologist Herb Krugman made the case that most people do not pay as much active attention to TV ads as, for example, print ads.[7] They might stare at them passively, perhaps whilst thinking of other things, if they even look at them at all. People do not generally believe that ads are going to tell them much useful information about a product, so they do not consciously scrutinize ads. For ad man turned psychologist Robert Heath, these apparent weaknesses of TV ads are actually their secret strength. He makes the case that TV advertising works by going under the radar of our rational, critical attention, and speaking directly to the irrational non-conscious.[8] The effect is on our non-conscious minds (specifically on something called 'implicit memory', which we look at more closely in Chapter 7).

Subliminal and supraliminal attention

Subliminal stimuli are those that are presented too quickly for our conscious, rational minds to be aware of. For example, an image flashed on a screen for less than 100 milliseconds. There is some evidence that shows subliminal messages can nudge but not force us to do things. Subliminal messaging can increase the chances that we will do something that is already within our repertoire of behaviours we might consider. For example, you can be made to be feel more thirsty, or to choose a particular brand of drink, but you cannot be made to feel thirsty *and* want a particular brand of drink.

However, whilst subliminal messaging may not be as powerful as many people believe, there is probably a lot more influence from what is known as supraliminal messaging. Whilst subliminal stimuli are not consciously seen, supraliminal stimuli are things that can be seen once our attention is drawn to them. It is likely that supraliminal stimuli are far more prevalent and influential in marketing than subliminal stimuli. For example, with TV ads we can, if we choose, pay very close attention to them and perceive all their details – it's just that we usually choose not to.

Memory

One of the key differences for marketers is that between recall and recognition. If a researcher asks you to name all the ads you saw on TV last night, this is recall. If, instead, they play you a series of ads and ask if you saw any of them last night, this is recognition. It is probably obvious that recognition is easier than recall. Our brains evolved to be great at recognizing things in our immediate environment, but there was not such a strong evolutionary pressure to become good at freely recalling information if it wasn't being 'cued up' by current stimuli around us. Not only is recognition easier than recall, its capacity seems to be far greater.[9]

Long-term memory is of especial relevance to marketing. Brands are essentially memories: a range of stimuli, concepts and emotions that we associate together. These sets of associations are not necessarily rational, or even conscious. They probably accumulate just through repetition. For example, the more often we hear a particular word used in association with a brand, the closer the memory link between the two and the more likely one is to prime the other.

A brand consists of a network – or web – of memories. Some of these will trigger the brand, other are more likely to come to mind once you have already thought of the brand. Byron Sharp and Jenni Romaniuk have coined the term 'mental availability' (also sometimes called 'brand salience') to refer to the power of a brand's memory web to bring it to mind in buying situations (eg at the supermarket shelf, the department-store counter, or when sitting at your computer, about to search for a product or service online).[10] This is not quite the same thing as 'top of mind' awareness, a metric that marketers often measure just through a single cue, such as the product category (eg 'What brands of soft drink can you recall?'). Mental availability is made up of the number and quality (strength) of relevant cues that might come into play when a person is about to make a purchase. These cues can be with a logo, packaging, the consumption experience, the context of purchase or consumption, or need states.

Peak–end rule

Our memories of emotional experiences are different from the emotional experiences themselves. Two things primarily influence how we remember how we felt about a past experience: how we felt at its peak, and how we felt when it ended.[11] The length of time that we felt pleasure or pain does not seem to be so important. For example, you might think that if a person experienced 10 minutes of a pleasurable experience, they would be left with a memory of having twice as much pleasure as a person who only went through five minutes of the same level of pleasure. This may be of relevance in measuring reactions to ads, where it might be more meaningful to look at the highest peak and the end of people's reactions than to a global average of the whole experience.

The Zeigarnik effect

Unfinished things tend to linger in our memory more than things that are completed. For example, waiters tend to remember the orders of customers who haven't yet paid more than those who have. Possible implications are that ads that tell a story in a series across a number of ads may be more memorable over time; ads that leave elements unresolved may also be more memorable. Similarly, the composer and author Leonard Bernstein argued that ambiguity is a powerful feature in art. By leaving unanswered questions and ambiguities in a painting, story or film, the artist invites the viewer or reader's own mind to 'fill in the blanks', creating an experience that may be more personally involving and perhaps even lingers in their non-conscious mind long after they have been exposed to it.[12]

Primacy and recency

When presented with a series of pieces of information (such as key points in a story in an ad, or feature lists of products), we tend to be most likely to remember the first and last items. Sometimes called the 'serial position' effect, this is one of the oldest findings in psychology. It may be of use in marketing when presenting lists of information, but might be less relevant to the flow of information presented in an ad, as other features of the ad (such as emotions created during its sequence) can bias what we are likely to remember from it.

Working memory

In-between memory and attention is our working memory. This is the number of bits of information that we can hold in our mind and think about at once – like the desktop of our conscious mind. The maximum capacity of our working memory is often called 'cognitive load'. Beginning with research in the 1950s, working memory capacity was proposed to be around seven chunks of information.[13] More recent work places it at around four chunks. Similarly, and particularly relevant to usability design (eg menus on websites), is Hick's law, which states that the time taken to make a decision tends to increase logarithmically the more options that are given.

The other constraint is that we can only easily process one stream of words at a time, so, for example, voice-overs on an ad should not clash with other text on-screen (although simultaneous presentation of the same words in on-screen text and voice-over can be effective).

Emotion

Whilst attention and memory are important for information processing, it is our emotions that have the upper hand in motivating us and attracting us to buy one brand or product over another. Emotions (from the Latin word *emovere*, meaning to move) are almost certainly evolutionarily ancient mechanisms to get us to move. For example, fear is a powerful motivator to move away from danger. Given the power of the emotions to motivate, it is no surprise that they are not only of interest to marketers, but of key importance in understanding apparently irrational consumer behaviours.

Whilst you might think that something as fundamental as emotion would be well understood by scientists, you might be surprised at how many areas of contention there still are. For example, there are debates about the extent to which emotions are inbuilt biological phenomena, versus cultural or learned, and, related to this, the extent to which emotions are caused by non-conscious bodily reactions rather than by cognitive processes that are attempting to decode what is going on around us. All we can really say at this point, on both debates, is that it is a mixture. For example, whilst there appear to be at least some universal emotions, there also seems to be a lot of variation in the way that people express emotions, and, particularly with the more secondary, social emotions, a number of cultural specific ones. It is also clearly the case that emotions are often accompanied by physiological changes, such as increasing heart rate, sweating, muscle tension etc (see Chapter 8 for more on measuring these), yet there are not definitive distinct physio-markers for each emotion. The key point is that emotions (or feelings) are a complex interplay of conscious/non-conscious, physiological and social forces, and pulling apart the effect of each is not always easy.

Some researchers distinguish between emotion as a physiological response, and the psychological experience of feeling. We may have an emotion without being consciously aware of it and, hence, forces that are not under the control of our rational awareness can motivate us.

Ways that consumers are affected non-consciously emotionally include:

- *Mood congruent recall*: when we are in a particular mood, be it positive or negative, our thinking and choices change. For example, we are more likely to recall happy memories when we are feeling happy, and vice versa for sad memories.

- *Positive associations*: repeatedly pairing a brand with positive emotions rubs off, and creates a halo of good feelings around it. This is completely irrational if we stop to think about it, but the point is that we so rarely do!

- *Environmental emotional boosters*: in-store environments are increasingly finding ways to put shoppers in a more relaxed, positive and indulgent mood. For example, scents pumped into the air can be used to create a certain mood, or stimulate appetite. Music has an effect on purchasing behaviour (for example, in one study, when shoppers could hear classical music in the alcohol section of a supermarket, they on average purchased more expensive bottles of wine).

Consumers probably find it hard to put their feelings about brands and products into words, not because they don't have the vocabulary, but because free recall is harder than recognition. In Chapter 7 we see how we can use this insight to measure consumers' associations with a brand, design or ad by prompting them with emotional words, rather than by asking them to recall them.

Embodied cognition

In order to cope with the continuous deluge of incoming sensory impressions humans also evolved ways of thinking that involve our bodies. After all, we are not just abstract minds, we sense and interact with our environment through our bodies. *Embodied cognition* is a fancy new term for saying that we often think with our bodies in mind.

A good example is playing tennis. When you are standing on the court and your opponent hits the ball at you at 100 miles per hour how do you know – in the split second available to you – where to run to meet it? Is your brain performing an abstract calculation of trajectories and speed? It turns out that there is a body movement shortcut at work; if the person fixes their gaze on the ball then begins to run and adjusts their speed until the accelerating ball looks like it is actually moving at a constant speed, they end up in the right place to meet it.

Equally, we often pull on memories of bodily movements and sensations when thinking about how things make us feel. We talk about something 'pulling us in', making us 'sick to our stomachs', of a person being 'cold' or 'warm', of 'jumping into' a decision, 'carrying a heavy load' or 'grasping an idea'. Language metaphors that tap into such bodily movements and sensations can be highly powerful with consumers.

Our own bodily sensations can also directly affect our judgements. Psychologists have found that when people are asked to rate the personality of a stranger who had previously asked them to hold a hot drink, they were more likely to rate them as a 'warm person' than if they had been asked to hold a cold drink.[14] Even our own posture and muscle movements can influence us. For example, psychologists have found that when the muscles that people use to smile are tensed (by asking people to hold a pencil between their teeth), they are more open to be amused when reading a humorous sentence. Also, some research shows that the movements we make with our mouths when saying particular words can influence the feelings and associations we have with those words.

For example, consider the following imaginary words: 'malooma', 'bouba', 'kiki' and 'taketi'. Now imagine that two of the words describe objects that are large and curved, whilst the other two describe things that are small and pointy or angular. Which would you guess are which?

Most people instinctively feel that malooma and bouba should describe large round objects, whilst kiki and taketi describe small pointy ones. This is because of the fact that we have to make a larger opening with our mouths to say words like 'malooma' (just as with words like 'enormous' and 'huge') whilst words like 'kiki' involve smaller openings, and – like words 'mini', 'petite' and 'tiny' – involve stretching our lips to make small openings. It seems that many words probably evolved because they naturally 'sound' like the thing they are describing, due to the way they make our mouths feel.[15]

Such responses can lead to irrational choices, yet are a by-product of deeply ingrained ways of thinking that we use all the time. As well as underlining the importance of bodily feedback and using metaphors to talk to your consumers' non-conscious, embodied thinking shows how important it can be to work across all senses.

Neuroscientist Antonio Damasio, in books such as *Descartes' Error* (1994), argued that our rational thinking is always informed by our emotions.[16] The two are rarely ever completely separate modes of thinking. Even when we don't feel that we are in a highly emotional state, our emotions can still be exerting a subtle pull on our decision-making. Damasio's 'somatic marker' hypothesis argues that we evaluate things on the basis of how they make our bodies feel (hence people whose smile muscles are activated find themselves more amused). These 'gut feelings' do not always override our rational judgements, but rather work in tandem with them, helping us to refine down the range of options under consideration, or warn us of a bad decision. These feelings can pop into our consciousness although we might not know the reason as to why we feel that way. For example, in one experiment Damasio got participants to play a card gambling game, presenting them with two decks of cards to choose from. Without them knowing, one deck was 'rigged' to offer bad cards. Intriguingly, the participants seemed to become intuitively aware (system 1) of the nature of the bad deck before they were consciously aware. Biometric measures (more about these in Chapter 9) showed a bodily stress response when their hands hovered over the bad deck, which was not present when they were about to choose from the good deck!

Attention, memory and emotion are three of the main mental constructs that neuromarketers use in understanding non-conscious data. In Chapter 3 we look more specifically at why consumers find certain things attractive.

Summary

- Our attention is limited, and hence we require a lot of non-conscious processing to 'fill in the gaps'. This means that assumptions and memories bias our perception.

- Our ability to recognize is far stronger than our ability to recall. Brands consist of a web of non-conscious memories.

- Emotions are a key motivating factor that likely evolved to get us to move (eg away from danger or towards opportunities for things such as food).

Notes

1 For example, one study found that simply including an fMRI brain image in a scientific paper increased its ratings of 'scientific reasoning' above the same paper not having a brain image. McCabe, DP and Castel, AD (2008) Seeing is believing: the effect of brain images on judgements of scientific reasoning, *Cognition*, **107** (1), pp 343–52.

2 Shepard, RN (1984) Ecological constraints on internal representation: resonant kinematics of perceiving, imagining, thinking and dreaming, *Psychological Review*, **91** (4), pp 417–47.

3 James, W [1890] (1983) *The Principles of Psychology*, vol. 1, Harvard University Press, Cambridge, MA, pp 403–4.

4 Simons, DJ and Chabris, CF (1999) Gorillas in our midst: sustained inattentional blindness for dynamic events, *Perception*, **28**, pp 1059–74.

5 Swallow, KM, Zacks, JM and Abrams, RA (2009) Event boundaries in perception affect memory encoding and updating, *Journal of Experimental Psychology: General*, **138**, pp 236–57.

6 Adam Brasel, S and Gips, J (2008) Breaking through fast-forwarding: brand information and visual attention, *Journal of Marketing*, **72** (6), pp 31–48.

7 Krugman, HE (1965) The impact of television advertising: learning without involvement, *Public Opinion Quarterly*, **29** (Fall), pp 349–56.

8 Heath, R (2012) *Seducing the Subconscious*, Wiley-Blackwell, London.

9 Research by Lionel Standing in the early 1970s suggested that our capacity to recognize images that we have seen before may be almost limitless. See Standing, L (1973) Learning 10,000 pictures, *Quarterly Journal of Experimental Psychology*, **25** (2), pp 207–22.

10 Sharp, B (2010) *How Brands Grow*, Oxford University Press, Melbourne.

11 This is covered in: Kahneman, D (2011) *Thinking, Fast and Slow*, Penguin, London.

12 From a series of lectures given by Leonard Bernstein at Harvard University in 1973 titled 'The Unanswered Question'. Available [Online] https://www.youtube.com/watch?v=hwXO3I8ASSg [accessed 24 April 2015].

13 Miller, GA (1956) The magical number seven plus or minus two: some limits on our capacity for processing information, *Psychological Review*, **63** (2), pp 81–97. And:Cowan, N (2001) The magical number 4 in short-term memory: a reconsideration of mental storage capacity, *Behavioral and Brain Sciences*, **24**, pp 87–185.

14 Williams, L and Bargh, J (2008) Experiencing physical warmth promotes psychological warmth, *Science*, **322**, pp 606–7.

15 Gómez Milán, E, Iborra, O, de Córdoba, MJ, Juárez-Ramos, V, Rodríguez Artacho, MA and Rubio, JL (2013) The kiki-bouba effect: a case of personification and ideaesthesia, *The Journal of Consciousness Studies*, **20** (1–2), pp 84–102.

16 Damasio, AR (1994) *Descartes' Error: Emotion, Reason and the Human Brain*, Random House, New York.

NEUROAESTHETICS 03

Anyone who has seen Stanley Kubrick's psychological horror film *The Shining* (1980) cannot help but be unnerved by its almost primal atmosphere of unease. Most viewers assigned its power to Jack Nicholson's performance of an alcoholic father going crazy while holed-up in a snowbound hotel. Yet it was not until years later that an additional secret of its psychological power to unnerve was discovered. A video-game designer, working on an entry in the 'Duke Nukem' series, was attempting to create a level of the game based on *The Shining*'s Overlook hotel. Yet as he attempted to map the building it became clear that it was physically impossible. Windows apparently looking outside had, in reality, corridors behind them; the ballroom was too large to fit the space allocated on the map; and some of the walls did not line up. When watching the film most people wouldn't consciously notice these things. When confronted with this strange fact in 2012, the executive producer finally admitted: 'The set was very deliberately built to be offbeat and off the track... the audience is deliberately made to not know where they're going. It's not supposed to make sense.'[1]

Of course, feeling fear when watching what we know to be a fictional story on a cinema or TV screen is itself irrational. Does advertising – be it on TV, the internet, posters or print – have similar powers to work on our non-conscious minds? If so, how does it do this, and what are its limits? Indeed, by looking at non-conscious processes can we also understand more about packaging, product design and in-store communications?

There is a range of guidelines that we can derive from research on the irrational non-conscious that point to ways in which commercial design and communications of all kinds can be enhanced, and marketing and advertising research can be used to better understand people's reactions to these.

When conducting neuro-research with consumers the actual data you get back is only half the story. You need to have ways to explain why consumers responded as they did. Just asking them (for the reasons discussed in Chapter 1) is not enough. However, the range of what we might call 'neuro-principles' that can help craft communications that engage and fascinate consumers can also help us explain the results we get from neuro-research. When applied to research these ideas can have a virtuous-cycle effect: they can help create more effective communications, then help inform and explain more insightful research, which can then help create even better communications, and so on.

This chapter can be read both as a range of principles that can be used even without doing any new research, and as a range of potential hypotheses and explanations for your own research. Obviously, cognitive neuro-science and psychology are large, ever-growing areas, and there are new things to learn and apply all the time. However, the principles that I will outline in this chapter have been selected on the basis of Pareto's law: there are always a minority of causes that account for the majority of effects. These principles have wide application, and also create a good framework of understanding that, no doubt, a lot of future findings will align with.

Our visual system is so important that a large area of our brains is dedicated to it. As there is such a one-to-one mapping of the visual field and visual features, scientists have gained a lot of knowledge over how it works. A growing new field of study called neuroaesthetics looks at how and why the brain finds certain things beautiful.[2] Some of the things we find beautiful are easily accounted for by thinking again of how our brains evolved. For example, there is a cross-cultural predilection for scenes of nature: in photographs, paintings and real views of things such as forests, fields and lakes – all things that would have been seen as signs of rich sources of food by our ancestors' brains. Less straightforward is why we also like more abstract visuals such as polka-dot patterns or abstract art. Some neuroscientists argue that the reason we like abstract patterns is because our brains get small jolts of pleasure by seeing clear, pure examples of shapes, colours and patterns that they are constantly trying to perceive within the much messier and more chaotic environment of the real world. For example, in everyday life when we view objects under imperfect or changing light conditions, and angles that may give us an obscured or distant view of an object, our brains have to work harder to figure out the real colours and patterns of the object. So finally 'locking-on' and perceiving the pattern clearly may be a little bit like the first sip of a drink when feeling thirsty: a small moment of satisfaction. As the psychologist Steven Pinker writes:

> We seem to get pleasure out of looking at purified, concentrated versions of the geometric patterns that in dilute form give us pips of microsatisfaction as we orient ourselves towards informative environments and fine-tune our vision to give us a clear picture of them.[3]

A similar effect may also be at work with music and sounds. Whilst some sounds denote very particular things, and lyrics can tell a story, much sound and music is abstract: it doesn't emotionally affect us by directly describing something.

Beauty

As well as finding natural scenes attractive, we also seem to have inbuilt biases towards other visual forms in what we find attractive. There are a number of inbuilt visual heuristics, and quirks of our visual cortex that lead us to either process certain images more fluidly (and hence appeal to our brain's desire to conserve energy), or lead us to find certain visuals more beautiful and/or pleasing to look at. In particular:

- We have dedicated neuro-modules for decoding faces, and are drawn to looking at faces and finding them emotionally engaging.[4]

- Due to the fact that the left hemisphere of our cortex receives information from our right visual field fractions of a second before our right cortex (and vice versa for the right hemisphere and left half of our visual field), and our left hemisphere does more language processing, and our right more image processing, we have a natural bias towards seeing text to our right and images to our left. For example, one study showed that people preferred ads in which the images were on the left and text on the right,[5] and another found that people were more likely to remember packages when the images/text were arranged that way.[6] The effect may only occur in right-handed people (who make up at least 7 out of 10 of the population), as this right–left specialization is not so marked in left-handers.

FIGURE 3.1   Which bar is darker: the top or bottom?

- A similar effect, called pseudoneglect, is that we pay more attention to things in the left side of our visual field than the right. This means that we exaggerate image elements such as darkness or lightness: as can be seen in Figure 3.1: more people see the top bar as darker, even though the bottom bar is simply a flipped-over version of the top one. Their brains are exaggerating the darkness on the left of the top one and the lightness on the left of the bottom one. We also are more likely to bump into things on our right side, and when actors wish to enter a theatre stage unseen by the audience they will do so on the right.

- As artists and designers have long believed, certain mathematical symmetries and proportions (such as designs that conform to the 'golden ratio') are deemed to be naturally more beautiful. It is possible that roots to such preferences are hard-wired in our brains (see Chapter 11 for more on this).

- Interfaces that are rated as more beautiful are experienced as having greater usability.[7]

We tend to find things beautiful if they are easy for our brains to process (more on this shortly).

Faces

Few things in our visual environments hold as much interest and meaning for us as faces. Film director John Ford said, 'The most interesting landscape is the human face.' The face communicates a rich array of information about a person's identity, their intentions and especially their emotions. We often non-consciously mirror the facial expressions of others, bringing us into close empathic connection with them: helping us feel what they are feeling.

It is therefore not surprising that we look to images of faces, be they in point-of-sale material, posters or packaging, to provide meaning. Faces are a shortcut to emotional engagement. For example, if we see a face looking at another person, directly at the camera, or at some other feature of the picture, it can draw us in emotionally and guide our own gaze. Yet if we see a face merely looking off into the distance, it may be far less engaging. One example of how faces can be used to emotionally engage us is a technique often used by film director Steven Spielberg. He will show us a person's face that we know is looking at something we are interested in. The camera will linger on their face for a little longer than usual – as the tension grows to see what they are looking at, we cannot help but be drawn into empathy with them, trying to read what they are seeing from their facial reactions. Finally, on revealing what they are looking at we are more engaged with it than we would otherwise have been.

In terms of screens, faces work particularly well on TVs and cinema screens, but may lack some of the detail and nuance that help us empathize and engage with them when they are depicted on small screens such as on a mobile phone. Given the increasing ubiquity of mobile phones in accessing the web and video sites such as YouTube, this may be a challenge for advertisers, and they should at least consider making faces particularly clearly visible in ads that may be seen on the smallest screens.

Colours

Colours do not just have effects of their own, but also act as markers to help us identify brands. Some brands become closely identified with very specific colour hues. For example, the royal purple of Cadbury or the bright lime green of Garnier. This makes them more distinctive and easier to find on-shelf – a good example of Byron Sharp's 'mental availability' concept mentioned in Chapter 2.

It has been estimated that around 8 per cent of men and 0.5 per cent of women have some form of colour-blindness:[8] an inability or diminished ability to perceive differences between certain colours (the most frequent type is the inability to distinguish between any colours that are composed of red or green). This has obvious implications for the distinctiveness and fluency of visual designs. There are websites where you can upload and quickly check what an image will look like to someone with different forms of colour-blindness.

Culture

When it comes to top-down processing, culture plays a big role. We may all have the same basic 'design' of brain at birth, and the language of the brain is the same the world over, but the patterns we learn, and hence the meanings we apply to things and contexts, can be very different. What is funny in China, for example, may not be as funny in Europe, and vice versa. Acquired tastes and cultural meanings obviously differ between countries, and for this reason the research considerations for the irrational consumers' minds are the same as traditional research.

For example, in many Asian cultures there is greater emphasis on understanding the context of a scene, compared to Western cultures that instead highlight the focus or subject of a scene. In one study, students at universities in the United States and Japan were shown several short animated underwater scenes that included multiple elements such as moving fish, rocks, bubbles, vegetation etc.[9] The participants were asked to describe what they had seen in each scene. Whilst the Japanese students were just as likely as their US counterparts to describe the main imagery of the moving fish, they were more likely to also describe background and contextual elements of the scene. They were then shown a number of images and asked which images showed fish they had previously seen from the video clips. In some of the images there were fish they had seen before but with slightly different backgrounds, whilst sometimes there were fish they had seen before but with the same backgrounds. The Japanese students were more likely to recognize the fish when it was shown in its original background than a new one, suggesting that they had processed the whole image holistically, unlike the US students, who were equally likely to recognize the fish in either the original or a novel environment.

Eight neuro-principles and their implications

The following are a selection of neuro-design principles. They are not the only ones that are used by consumer-neuroscience practitioners, but are among those most frequently used:

- processing fluency;
- familiarity = liking;
- priming;
- the peak-shift effect;
- threat/attraction motivation;
- associative memory webs;
- multi-sensory integration;
- empathy and mirroring.

The overriding theme of most of these is that of making designs easy for the brain to process. The brain is an energy-hungry part of the body – and conscious, deliberative thought in particular seems to burn energy. From an evolutionary standpoint minimizing energy consumption is beneficial because it lowers the possibility of the person starving to death. Therefore, the brain has evolved myriad shortcuts (often termed heuristics, particularly in the context of how we assign value to things – see Chapter 4 for more on this) for performing its functions with minimal energy. As consumers we become habitual, and whenever possible avoid making conscious, rational calculations over most purchases, preferring to rely on mental shortcuts, intuition and our emotions.

Processing fluency

Neuroscientists studying how easy it is to process things like images call it processing fluency. A number of features of images have been found to increase their processing fluency and also tend to make us like the images more or find them more beautiful/attractive.[10] The effects of processing fluency have also been captured directly; images that are easier to process have been found to be more likely to briefly activate the muscles we use to smile than harder-to-process images (and were not associated with the muscles we use to frown).[11] The key features are:

- Figural goodness: how well the overall structure or composition of the image makes it easy to understand what we are seeing. This can often be seen in the eye-tracking gaze-plots of an image: whether there is an integrated flow or concentration of view on the image, or whether people's eyes are moving all over it, not knowing where to focus.

- Figure–background contrast: how easy it is to see the foreground or most important subject of the image against the background.

- Stimulus repetition: an image can be complex, but if it has repeating patterns it makes it easier to process.

- Symmetry: repetition of pattern or shape around an axis of reflection. We find symmetry around a vertical axis easier to process than around a horizontal one. Hardest of all is symmetry around a diagonal axis (but still easier than a non-symmetrical shape or pattern) (see Figure 3.2).

- Prototypicality: how much the image represents an average or typical instance of its type.

FIGURE 3.2   Different angles of symmetry: vertical, horizontal and diagonal

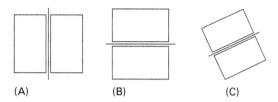

(A)   (B)   (C)

Whilst these features tend to make images easier to process, they also have to be tempered with several caveats. First, the more familiar we are with looking at something, the easier it is for us to process. For example, those with art training are less likely to prefer the simplicity of symmetrical shapes than the average person.

Second, processing fluency is more likely to result in positive feelings if we expect the information to be hard to understand and it turns out to be easy. Good examples of this are well-designed infographics, where the designer manages to illustrate complex information in an intuitive and easy-to-grasp way.

Some other ways to make marketing material more effortless to decode are:

- Stories and metaphors: information presented in terms of stories or metaphors often makes it more human and easy to digest, as well as making it more engaging. For example, language that is sensory-rich and evokes mental images or memories of sensations, such as scents or pleasing tactile experiences, can be easier to process.

- Clear to read: is your font easy to read? Does the colour of your text stand out well against the background? (White text on a black background can be hard to read, for example.) Read your copy aloud to check whether it flows easily or sounds awkward.

- Clear to see: if you are using graphics, aim to keep to less than four visual clusters. Our brains can immediately decode up to around this number of items, but any more and we have to put in extra effort to take them in. This probably came from the evolutionary pressures on our ancestors, when coming across a number of predatory animals, to know whether our hunting group outnumbers them (hence they are an opportunity to hunt) or they outnumber us (hence they are a risk to run from). One way to check the clarity of a design is to test whether it is still understandable at a smaller size. For example, shoppers will not always be viewing a poster or in-store display at the optimum distance and viewing angle.

- Rhythm and rhyming: ad jingles may be seen as retro or simplistic, but they tap into a powerful human predilection for rhythm and rhyme in speech. If a sentence rhymes, it not only makes it more memorable and easy to digest, but can also make it more persuasive.

- Repetition and familiarity: using elements that are familiar to your consumers, or making sure that they see your message a lot, will help make it smoother for them to process.

- Minimizing cognitive load: we all have a limited working memory span, so make sure that you do not make too many demands on consumers' attention in one go. This is particularly relevant to tasks such as getting them to fill in forms or order things online.

- Sensory syllables: in the same way that words have syllables, concepts and other sensory stimuli have a notional 'amount of complexity' that translates into the amount of time and effort a person has to devote to processing them. For example, double negatives such as 'it is not entirely unnatural' are harder to process than more direct expressions: 'it is natural'.

- The power of three: our brains have an inbuilt ability to recognize up to around three or four objects or visual clusters, after which we have to work harder to count each one. This comes from the evolutionary imperative to be able to quickly size up whether or not we are likely to be outnumbered by a group of predators. Our ability to seemingly instantly process up to three items is known as subitizing.[12] This probably often translates into designs (posters, packaging designs etc.) with simple arrays of four or fewer clusters being easier to process. As students of rhetoric know, three is also powerful in verbal persuasion. It has a feeling of 'completeness' about it, so much so that we feel uncomfortable just mentioning two things, and will often use a verbal 'filler' such as 'and so on' or 'etc' in order to bulk out a list of two things into a list of three. Speech givers also use it as a 'clap-trap'.

So the overriding theme is that easier to process is better. Below are some principles that mainly flow directly from this, or are different instances of it.

Familiarity = liking

Neuro-principle

Our brains mix up familiarity with liking. We have evolved a preference for things we have been exposed to before. After all, if they didn't kill us the first time, how bad can they be? Psychologists have identified something called the 'mere exposure effect': the tendency for people to rate things as more positive if they have seen them before.[13] Another effect, called the 'halo effect', is that people often generalize one positive feature of a person or thing into interpreting or assuming that they have other positive characteristics too. For example, a person viewed as attractive will also more likely be assumed to have other positive characteristics such as higher than average intelligence.

Consumer implications

If a brand generates goodwill with one product, it may rub off on its other products. Also, familiarizing consumers with your brand, product and packaging in advertising and communications can make them better disposed towards it in-store just because of familiarity (ie not because they are rationally persuaded).

Novelty versus familiarity

One apparent paradox here is that whilst familiarity is generally positive, novelty can also be a powerful tool for drawing the eye. For example, visual images that are impossible, or create visual jokes of some kind, can stop us in our tracks and cause us to look at a poster ad, for example, for just that little bit longer than usual and, like a joke, can give us that little hit of pleasure as the novelty or ambiguity is resolved and we 'get' it. Alternatively, there might be no resolution and the ambiguity leaves us hanging, with unresolved tension that can worm its way into our nonconscious mind. However, we also probably evolved a suspicion of novelty as new things could be threatening (whereas we have already learned whether familiar things are positive or not).

Novelty, by definition, is the opposite of familiarity. If both are effective, how are we to resolve their opposition? To some extent getting this balance right is a part of communication and design that falls within the realm of 'art': it is not always possible to predict. Our brains may have conflicting feelings about novelty: on one hand, novel things may be viewed with suspicion and a potential threat, on the other they may be a source of useful new information.

However, there are some guidelines to think about. The effect of novelty is to grab and hold the eye, and hence also increase our conscious awareness. In an in-store environment this can be very important, but should be done in a way that doesn't violate the distinctiveness and recognizability of a package or branded display. For posters, novelty can be particularly potent as it is so easy for us not even to see a poster, particularly outdoors, even within the supraliminal attention of our peripheral vision. TV ads can also use novelty to attract and hold visual attention, which might otherwise wander as the person considers fast-forwarding or otherwise avoiding watching the ads. Online banner ads may benefit from novelty if their primary goal is to grab conscious attention and get the web browser to click. But if the aim is to increase awareness and familiarity, it might be best to avoid novelty.

Also, some marketing communications need to get people to rethink old assumptions, so violating their expectations can work favourably here.

Priming

Neuro-principle

The brain's cortex can be thought of as a prediction maker or pattern detector. It is continually non-consciously scanning its environment to predict what might happen next. This means that information that we have recently been exposed to looms larger in our thinking and decision-making than non-present information. Equally, information that can easily be brought to mind (either because it is familiar or it is easy to visualize) tends to have a more powerful effect on us than information that is more abstract or harder to visualize – hence people are more likely to be scared of a terrorist incident (easy to visualize) than heart disease (hard to visualize).

Associative priming is an example of this and is an important concept in neuromarketing. Whenever we are exposed to an idea or stimulus, be it an ad, brand logo or package design, all the concepts that are closely associated to that thing become non-consciously primed in our minds, in other words they become more readily accessible and come to mind more easily. It is analogous to a good personal assistant who discreetly pulls out all the related files on a particular client when they phone up, just in case the files are needed quickly. (There will be more on priming in Chapter 7.)

Consumer implications

Advertising and marketing messages may work better the nearer (in time and space) they are delivered to the point of purchase. The more that certain colours, sounds, concepts and images are paired with a brand or product, the more likely they will become accessible to the person whenever they are exposed to the brand.

Non-conscious motivation

New research since the mid-1990s has shown that whilst consumers are motivated by goals, they are not always consciously aware of this, or of where those goals have come from. Goal templates already exist in consumers' minds. For example, we might have models for goals such as 'I want to indulge myself with something expensive or pleasurable' or 'I want to save money and buy a basic option or a bargain'. We can consciously, rationally choose to pursue one of those two contrasting goals, but they can also be triggered by environmental cues.

For example, in one study the researchers exposed the participants to a series of brand names either associated with indulgence and prestige (such as Tiffany, the jewellery retailer) or with money-saving thriftiness (such as Walmart).[14] The brand names were presented just outside their conscious awareness (by being flashed very quickly just outside their central visual focus). They were then asked to choose a brand of socks and a brand of microwave from a range of options. Those who had been non-consciously exposed to the luxury brand names were more likely to choose more expensive options than those who had been exposed to the thrifty brand names. Further, when carefully questioned about their choices afterwards, the participants were completely oblivious to the possibility that they might have been influenced non-consciously.

Our behaviour can also be primed in this way by environmental cues that non-consciously trigger stereotypes or personality-based models of behaviour. For example, when people are exposed to words that relate to the stereotypes of old age they subsequently walk more slowly, even though they may be unaware as to why.[15] However, the key difference is that these stereotype forms of priming tend to be short term and diminish over time, whereas non-conscious goals tend to increase in strength over time until the goal is met. Other research suggests that this type of brand-exposure effect can backfire when it comes to exposure to slogans.[16] If consumers are exposed to something that they have learned to associate with a persuasion tactic, such as a brand or advertising slogan, it can activate a non-conscious goal to resist it, resulting in behaviour that is counter to the aim of the slogan. Brand logos, however, are able to activate goals but are less likely to be perceived as a persuasion tactic and therefore less likely to create this type of negative priming.

Whilst these findings are still largely lab-based, it is reasonable to assume that similar effects could occur in the real world. For example, in-store if a shopper sees lots of signs that prime the goal of thrifty money-saving, it may make it harder to then shift them into a more indulgently driven shopping goal. Conversely, if there are environmental cues that trigger more indulgent goals, it may be easier to sell more expensive brands.

The peak-shift effect

Neuro-principle

When key, meaningful or distinguishing features of an image are exaggerated it can make the images easier to process. An example of this is that sometimes people can more quickly recognize a person from a caricature cartoon of them (which exaggerates their unique facial features) than a regular image of them. Even aside from caricatures, artists will often exaggerate the unique essence of something in order to make their artworks more striking.

Consumer implications

Important distinguishing elements of an image could be exaggerated to help consumers find it easier to process. Elements of product images, for example, can be exaggerated to help consumers recognize the aspects of them that are important to recognition. Brand mascots could be rendered in a more caricature format in some instances, or brand logos or other brand visuals illustrated in more exaggerated ways.

Threat/attraction motivation

Neuro-principle

This is not a direct example of processing fluency, but an important low-level emotional consideration. We are constantly, non-consciously scanning our environment for threats/opportunities. This is an obvious evolutionary adaptation as being able to avoid predators and find food are skills of supreme survival value. However, whilst the environment of the contemporary world is mostly free of the risks of predators and lack of food, these emotional programmes are still active within us.

Consumer implications

Designers of marketing materials, and advertisers, should be careful of elements that might (albeit non-consciously) remind consumers of a threat, and hence cause them to emotionally retract. For example, any imagery that could appear even mildly threatening or anxiety-arousing should be treated very carefully, particularly if it might become linked to your brand itself. Also, in-store designers should think about how to make displays and fixtures inviting to approach and navigate around without the appearance of sharp edges or overly angular corners.

Associative memory webs

Neuro-principle

Our memories are structured like a net of associations. When two things happen in close proximity (in time or space) to each other, our non-conscious begins to connect the two. This is particularly noticeable if we catch a sickness bug: we often feel disgust at the thought of the type of food we ate immediately before the bug struck – a feeling that can continue long after the sickness itself has gone. This process of connecting two things that occur in succession can be non-rational, such that if we hear a claim repeated about someone or something often enough our non-conscious may accept it, even if we rationally know that it cannot be the case if we stopped and consciously thought about it. (See Chapter 7 for more on these types of memory associations.)

Consumer implications

This principle offers us an explanation of how advertising can work: the simple but repeated pairing of concepts (such as a brand with an idea or an emotion) can become powerfully embedded in our memories, even if our conscious mind is not paying much attention to them (eg see Robert Heath's 'low involvement processing' model). Memory webs also give us a model for how brands exist in consumers' minds: as a series of associated concepts and sensory information.

Multi-sensory integration

Neuro-principle

As our brains are constantly comparing information from different senses in order to decode what is happening around us, more than one stream of sensory information communicating the same thing makes it easier for us.

Some of the most memorable moments in cinematic history have featured the clever marrying of sound and vision in this way. In *2001: A Space Odyssey* (1968) the slow majestic spinning of a space station is paired with a waltz (a form of music used for slowly spinning dancers). In Alfred Hitchcock's *Psycho* (1960) the knife-attack sequence in the shower is dramatically enhanced by a memorable score that not only suggested a high-pitched scream, but the staccato movements of a knife-stabbing. In Disney's *Fantasia* (1940) and *Fantasia 2000* (2000) the entire concept of the film is the creation of animated sequences that provide a direct visual expression of pieces of music.

Consumer implications

When creating TV or web ads, attention should be paid to getting the soundtrack to work in synch with the visuals. For example, if there is a voice-over at the end, ensure that it is not competing for the viewer's language-processing resources by saying something different from any text that is appearing at the same time.

Is there a good match between a product's name and its essential characteristics (eg the bouba/kiki effect mentioned in Chapter 2)?

Empathy and mirroring

Neuro-principle

We are a social species and have evolved in such a way that we try to understand the motivations and emotions of others. We often do this by 'putting ourselves in their shoes': ie running a mental simulation of how we would feel if we were in the same situation. Often just seeing an image of a person in a particular situation can trigger feelings in us as though we were also in that situation.

Consumer implications

Marketing materials depicting people interacting with an appealing moment of consuming a product, or engaged in interacting with others, can help trigger the same feelings and emotions in consumers.

Using neuro-principles

Why do you need these principles? Why don't the results of neuro-research speak for themselves? Most of the research described in this book will yield numerical or graphical-type results that will need some context to help it make sense. In essence, the numbers will tell you the 'what' but the context will tell you the 'why'. The context is the range of shortcuts that are made by our quirky irrational brains. These are the rules for how our brains process the world around us. Broadly speaking, I have split them into two types. First, the neuroaesthetic principles in this chapter are the shortcuts that relate to how we process sensory information and, in particular, visuals.

The second type of shortcuts is heuristics, which are typically more relevant to our judgements of price and value. We look at those more closely in the next chapter.

Summary

- Neuro-principles are features of our psychology that affect how we decode communications.

- Neuroaesthetics is a relatively new discipline that seeks insights from neuroscience into why we find certain things attractive.

- Seven key neuro-principles – which largely relate to processing fluency – are useful in understanding why commercial designs such as packaging or ads are effective with consumers.

Notes

1 Brooks, X (2012) [accessed 24 April 2015] Shining a Light in Room 237, *The Guardian*, 18 October [Online] http://www.theguardian.com/film/2012/oct/18/inside-room-237-the-shining.

2 Zeki, S (1999) Art and the brain, *Journal of Consciousness Studies: Controversies in Science and the Humanities*, **6**, pp 76–96.

3 Pinker, S (1998) *How the Mind Works*, Penguin, London.

4 Theeuwes, J (2010) Top-down and bottom-up control of visual selection, *Acta Psychologica*, doi: 10.1016/j.actpsy.2010.02.006.

5 Ellis, AW and Miller, D (1981) Left and wrong in adverts: neuropsychological correlates of aesthetic preference, *British Journal of Psychology*, **72** (2), pp 225–29.

6 Rettie, R and Brewer, C (2000) The verbal and visual components of package design, *Journal of Product & Brand Management*, **9** (1), pp 56–70.

7 Tractinsky, N, Katz, AS and Ikar, D (2000) What is beautiful is usable, *Interacting with computers*, **13**, pp 127–45.

8 Wong, B (2011) Color blindness, *Nature Methods*, **8** (6), p 441.

9 Study described in Nisbett, RE (2003) *The Geography of Thought: How Asians and Westerners think differently*, Nicholas Brealey, London.

10 Reber, R, Schwarz, N and Winkielman, P (2004) Processing fluency and aesthetic pleasure: is beauty in the perceiver's processing experience? *Personality and Social Psychology Review*, **8** (4), pp 364–82.

11 Winkielman, P and Cacioppo, JT (2001) Mind at ease puts a smile on the face: psychophysiological evidence that processing facilitation leads to positive affect, *Journal of Personality and Social Psychology*, **81**, pp 989–1000.

12 Butterworth, B (1999) *What Counts: How every brain is hardwired for math*, Free Press, London.

13 Zajonc, RB (2001) Mere Exposure: A gateway to the subliminal, *Current Directions in Psychological Science*, **10** (6), pp 224–28.

14 Chartrand, TL, Huber, J, Shiv, B and Tanner, RJ (2008) Nonconscious goals and consumer choice, *Journal of Consumer Research*, **35** (2), pp 189–201.

15 Bargh, JA, Chen, M and Burrows, L (1996) Automaticity of social behaviour: direct effects of trait construct and stereotype activation on action, *Journal of Personality and Social Psychology*, **71** (2), pp 230–44.

16 Laran, J, Dalton, AN and Andrade, EB (2011) The curious case of behavioral backlash: why brands produce priming effects and slogans produce reverse priming effects, *Journal of Consumer Research*, **37**, pp 999–1014.

BEHAVIOURAL ECONOMICS

04

Try to answer the following questions as quickly as possible:

1 If a cup of coffee and a cookie cost £4.80, and the coffee costs £4 more than the cookie, how much is the cookie?

2 Which are you more likely to do: drive an extra mile to save £5 on a purchase that would otherwise be £15 or to save £5 on a purchase that would otherwise be £400?

3 Assuming you are not on a diet and you want to treat yourself: your favourite bag of chocolates is now in a larger edition and on special offer. Which of the following two offers would make you more tempted to buy: '50% extra free' or 'Now 30% off'?

Of course, given that you are reading a book about the irrational consumer your suspicions will already have been raised that these questions might have been carefully crafted to catch you out. Hence your answers may have been more considered and rational than usual. Nevertheless, most people tend to give apparently irrational responses on at least one or more of the questions.

In question one, most people's minds will immediately jump to the answer that the biscuit must be worth 80p, as they are captured by the similarity between the £4 in the price and the mention of £4 more in the question. Yet the real answer is 40p! (Check it!)

In question two, considering this from a purely rational point of view, why would anyone think it is more worthwhile to drive an extra mile to save £5 on a £400 purchase than a £15 purchase? After all, the amount saved is exactly the same.

In question three, both of the ways of expressing the offer can refer to exactly the same deal! Overall, however, people tend to prefer the description '50% extra free' rather than '30% off', as the former sounds like a bonus, whilst the latter sounds like a bribe (why do they have to discount the product – can't they sell it?). Similarly, whilst neoclassical economic models would suggest that dropping price will typically increase sales, when we look at the way that consumers really behave we see that often this doesn't work. A price drop may signal that the product is of inferior quality or is unpopular, so the retailer has to drop the price in order to shift the stock.

What these example questions show is that when it comes to calculating prices, judging the value of price reductions and comparing the attractiveness of different offers, many of us much of the time don't think completely rationally. The field that examines these apparently irrational biases in our judgements of value is known as behavioural economics.

Value is not rationally objective

In order to make fully rational choices, almost every purchase decision would require an impractical amount of information-gathering and weighing-up. The neoclassical model of consumers performing Franklin-esque pros-and-cons analyses (as mentioned in Chapter 1) just isn't feasible in the real world.

One reason for this is that the value of a good or service is often subjective, and hence open to irrational interpretations. A particularly apposite example of this is wine. The price of a bottle of wine can vary enormously, and how is the average consumer to judge whether a bottle is worth the asking price? In the absence of a definitive and objective way of judging, consumers will resort to things such as contextual and social cues. Is the wine being served in a high-class restaurant? Or is it known to be an exclusive vintage? If so, we might feel that a higher price is more acceptable than if we were drinking a run-of-the-mill brand in a cheap restaurant. Whilst this may sound like an unremarkable observation, the interesting thing is that this effect seems to actually affect our perception of how much we enjoy a product. For example, in one experiment the participants were given two samples of a cola drink whilst in an fMRI brain scanner.[1] In some conditions they were told whether the drink was Coca-Cola or Pepsi, and in others they sampled them 'blind'. When participants were told the brands, they were more likely to say they preferred the Coca-Cola than the Pepsi when they tried them blind. Also, when they were told the brands there were patterns of brain activity seen in an area assumed to be involved in evaluating this brand information (the medial prefrontal cortex) that were not recorded in the blind-taste condition. Taken together, the self-reports and the change in brain activity were interpreted as showing that brand information could bias (favourably in this case) our taste perception. In another study, participants sampled five wines whilst in an fMRI scanner.[2] One of the samples they were told cost $5 a bottle, another $45. They were, however, exactly the same wine. When participants sampled the supposedly more expensive wine they reported a better taste than when they sampled the same wine under the lower price. The parts of their brains associated with higher expected taste pleasure (the medial orbitofrontal cortex) showed increased activity. Whilst these are only one type of product, the results suggest that price can create a higher expectation of quality, which then may influence our actual pleasure of consumption. Value, whilst experienced as real, can be altered by the information surrounding the experience.

The subjectivity of the price of an item is also influenced by the fact that consumers will often use relative proportions as their benchmark rather than absolute amounts. For example, the difference between two products priced at £100 and £200 will feel greater than that between two priced at £900 and £1,000 even though it is exactly the same. Yet in the second example the difference constitutes a smaller percentage of the overall value. Interestingly, we tend to put something that is 'free' in a completely different mental category, such that the difference between something that is free and something that costs £10 is probably perceived as even greater than a difference between £100 and £200. Our price perceptions are far from linear.

Equally, an experiment found that consumers were more likely to choose as desirable a pot of ice cream in which the pot was small and the ice cream was almost overflowing, rather than one in which the pot was so large that it had a lot of empty space and easily contained the ice cream, even though both had exactly the same volume of ice cream![3] Context and comparisons play a large role in our perception of value.

Not all spending is equal. For example, we often feel guilty if we spend our cash on treats or luxury items for ourselves, but less so if we use accumulated loyalty-card reward points or if someone else buys the item for us as a gift. It is not the consumption of the item that creates the guilt so much as the actual act of purchasing it. Consumers can have their pain of purchasing eased by giving them rational reasons to believe that a product or service is actually not frivolous or excessive to buy (eg information about its effectiveness, efficiency or to create a value-for-money comparison with a higher-priced alternative product). These reasonings can help them to consciously justify spending their money. Equally, consumers tend to treat spending on credit cards differently from spending the same amount in cash; and money that we had to work hard to obtain is spent more carefully than a sudden windfall.

What this means is that marketers need to think not just in terms of the emotional pleasure (or otherwise) of owning and consuming a product or service, but the pain or pleasure of the transaction itself. If the pain of the transaction process is putting off potential consumers, a simple change (or 'nudge', as described later in this chapter) could easily unlock many more sales.

Ecological rationality

Given the time, effort and imperfect information limitations on consumers' decision-making they tend to use the next best thing to rational thinking: bounded or ecological rationality.

Bounded rationality is a concept proposed by the polymath Herbert A Simon (1916–2001). His idea was that people attempt to act rationally but within the constraints of their own thinking and the information to which they have access. Ecological rationality is a similar idea, but emphasizes the influence of the environment on decision-making. Often, behaviour that seems irrational when measured by a purely abstract or arithmetic form of logic may be rational when viewed from the practical standpoint of what works for a person within the real world.

In other words, if we are not thinking clearly about the features of a person's environment we can attribute their behaviour to irrational internal choices, when actually it is nothing of the sort.

Simon was also a proponent of the idea of satisficing: as humans cannot always find the ultimate optimal choice, we instead tend to just seek the option that seems good enough. For example, sometimes it might be that the consumer has one particular feature that they don't want to compromise on, and as soon as they find a product that gives them this, they are comfortable with choosing it. Or it may be that there are several features that they need to satisfy, whilst they are willing to overlook others. Whilst there may be many reasons for the success of McDonald's, few would argue that it is down to superior quality of food, and most would accept that its consumers are largely satisficing by instead accepting a minimal threshold of quality in exchange for the benefits of consistency (their meals are predictably the same whenever they order them) and convenience. The trick is to find the key features that consumers want to have met, and those that they are willing to compromise on.

This is not to say that all consumers satisfice all of the time. For more important purchases such as a car or a computer they may invest extra effort into consciously weighing up features and options. Also some consumers are more thorough (or fussy!) in their regular shopping habits, wanting to put in above-average efforts to ensure they maximize their choices. Nevertheless, for most purchases, most of the time, consumers tend to take the path of least resistance, using system 1 thinking and defaulting to habit, what they know others are buying, or simply the market leader.

Bill Gates once said, 'I choose a lazy person to do a hard job. Because a lazy person will find an easy way to do it.' Similarly, our energy-stingy brains find a myriad of lazy system 1 ways to make value decisions. These are usually called heuristics. If, for example, a consumer is going to satisfice on a purchase choice, then they will be using some underlying heuristic to guide them.

The rise of behavioural economics

Despite the dominance of neoclassical economics, there have been a number of theorists who have incorporated more irrational forces into economic thinking.

For example, the Austrian school of economics, beginning around the 1920s, believed that economics should be viewed as a subset of psychology, not as one of the hard sciences like physics. Also, even Adam Smith, the 18th-century author of *The Wealth of Nations*, admitted the importance of some psychological factors in economic behaviour.

Nevertheless, a coherent model explaining the quirks of human economic decision-making did not begin forming until the 1970s. It was then that psychologists Daniel Kahneman and Amos Tversky began researching how people make economic decisions with less than perfect information. This resulted in a seminal paper, published in 1979, titled 'Prospect theory: an analysis of decision under risk'. Their theory describes the way that people weigh up potential gains and risks from a decision. Specifically, people do not view probabilities in a purely rational way, but have a tendency to overvalue low probabilities and undervalue high ones. They also described how people are loss averse, have a diminishing sensitivity to price differences (eg the difference between £100 and £200 feeling greater than that between £800 and £900), and tend to use anchor points of reference (against which they measure losses and gains).

The paper helped to launch the discipline of behavioural economics, for whose research in the field (and helping to integrate psychological findings into economics) Daniel Kahneman received the Nobel prize for economics in 2002. In recent years a number of popular books on the subject have made marketers more aware of it, and helped its adoption as a commercial tool.

Allied to the rise of behavioural economics has been the use of other behavioural science theories, such as game theory (explaining how people make decisions whilst weighing up the likely actions of others, incorporating such factors as fairness and reciprocity) and neuroeconomics (studying the neuroscience of decision-making).

Heuristics

Whilst there are numerous documented heuristics that influence consumer behaviour, below are seven of the most wide-ranging ones (see the notes section for some references to find more heuristics).

Loss aversion and the endowment effect

Heuristic

We are more sensitive to and motivated by fear of loss than prospect of gain. In the ancestral environment that our brains evolved in, it is easy to see how the pressures of that hunter-gatherer life would have led to this bias. Sources of food were always uncertain, and fear of starvation stalked our ancestors as much as the lions and other predators of the savannahs.

One strange consequence of this is that we tend to value things more highly once we already own them. This can even lead to some very strange behaviour. For example, once we have bought something, even if we then don't use it, we feel like it is a 'sunk cost', and therefore we are obliged to stick with it. Some people will even keep shoes that they never wear, until a certain period of time has passed that the shoes will have 'lost their value' and only then feel able to throw them away. To do so before would feel like a loss!

Consumer implications

Thirty-day trials or other 'try before you buy' schemes may increase the perceived value of a product in the consumer's eyes. Simply reminding consumers of 'benefits' they could gain may not always be as powerful as showing them how a product/service can help them protect what they already have.

Anchoring and framing

Heuristic

As value is often subjective, or at least ill-defined in the consumer's mind, other prices that they have seen or heard recently can act to set their expectations of a reasonable price. For example, as salespeople have always known, showing a prospective customer one or more higher-priced options will make a mid-range option – that they would otherwise perceive as too expensive – more reasonable. However, the effect is even stronger than you might think. Experiments have shown that merely mentioning or showing a number can influence people's numerical judgements soon afterwards. For example, in one experiment the participants were asked to use a roulette wheel that was, without them knowing, rigged to stop on either 10 or 65.[4] They were subsequently asked to estimate the percentage of United Nations members that were African countries. Those whose roulette number was 10 guessed on average 25 per cent whilst those whose ball hit 65 guessed 45 per cent. In another experiment, participants merely having to report their social security number subsequently affected people's estimate of the value of a bottle of wine (the lower their number, the lower the value).[5] This effect can also have implications for survey design. The psychologist Stuart Sutherland pointed out that people are drawn towards the middle figure when you ask them to rate something on a numerical scale, and the ranges of figures you give in a question can affect the responses you get.[6]

Consumer implications

How a product is displayed on-shelf can influence its perceived value. Shoppers will compare prices with adjacent products in order to perceive what is reasonable versus cheap/expensive. The introduction of more expensive variants in a category can help the other variants as it makes them seem more reasonably priced.

By making a (reasonable-sounding) comparison between a product/ service and a more expensive one (eg comparing a relaxing spa-morning to a beach holiday) you can shift people's frame of reference and make them happier about spending more. Even including a number in the communications for a product or service could influence consumers' perception of its price, particularly if it is a new product that doesn't yet have a determined value in the mind of consumers.

In contradiction to received wisdom, the anchoring effect can mean that it is best in a price negotiation to be the one who starts, and mentions the first price, which can then affect the perceptions of what is a reasonable expectation.

The affect heuristic and first impressions

Heuristic

When acquiring and weighing up all the necessary information to make a rational choice is just too much, we often just ask ourselves 'How do I feel about this option'? Typically we emotionally weigh up something new very quickly, and our judgements tend to be long-lasting. This is because we like to be consistent, so when beginning with a positive impression of something we subsequently seek and process information that confirms it (the same for a negative impression), a phenomenon known as the 'halo' effect. For this reason, first impressions – not just of people but of products, packaging and other communications – can be vastly dispropor-tionately influential. For example, one study found that web browsers formed an impression of the appeal of a web page in as little as 50 milli-seconds![7] However, because this happens at a largely non-conscious level (or only fleetingly passes through our consciousness) it can be hard to measure through asking questions, and is perhaps better meas-ured through non-conscious techniques (in particular, implicit response measures).

(Note: the power of first impressions can also be a form of anchoring – our first reference point with something determines how we calibrate our responses to it in the future.)

Consumer implications
Careful consideration should be paid to the introduction of a new product, package or campaign. As well as the details of a design (for example, of a web page), pay attention to the look and feel of the overall impression, or gestalt, as it is this that will be taken in during those first crucial milliseconds.

Thin-slicing

Thin-slicing is a term that psychologists use to describe the fact that we can sometimes make very fast non-conscious evaluations about things, which then result in uncannily accurate gut feelings. Our non-conscious minds can learn complex patterns and notice them quickly, even if we are consciously unaware of the underlying pattern. An example of this is a study that showed strangers who had viewed only several seconds of soundless video of a teacher were able to rate the teacher in a way that correlated with the ratings of students and supervisors who'd had many weeks of experience and interactions with the teacher.[8]

Social proof

Heuristic

Consumers will often look to others as a shortcut to making good buying decisions. If you know that others have bought something, it feels safer for you to do so, and in some instances you may want to make the same choices as others in order to give yourself something in common with them (eg giving a new best-selling paperback novel a whirl because everyone else is reading it). When shopping carts were originally invented in 1938 their creator, Sylvan Goldman, nudged reluctant shoppers to adopt them by paying people to push them around for a couple of years so that the behaviour seemed normal (by the time he passed away in 1984 he was worth $400 million!). The US electricity company Opower has successfully encouraged its users to save energy by giving them feedback on how their consumption compares to more energy-efficient households in their neighbourhood.[9]

Consumer implications

Remind consumers of the success of your product, particularly, where possible, of local success or of people 'like them' who have been using it. Don't emphasize the fact that others are doing a behaviour that you don't want. For example, don't say something like 'Still only 10 per cent of customers have discovered how great our new service is...'.

Availability

Heuristic

There are many heuristics that relate to our poor natural ability to judge statistical likelihoods. Our brains just did not evolve to think this way. Instead we tend to overestimate the likelihood of events that easily come to mind. For example, when asked if there are more words that begin with the letter 'K' than have it as their third letter, most of us tend to answer that there are more that begin with it. We answer this way purely because it is easier for us to think of examples of words that begin with 'K' than have it as their third letter (there are in fact more words in which 'K' appears as the third letter).

This is one of the reasons why well-known brands enjoy an advantage. When a consumer needs to buy something in a particular product or service category, particularly if they don't buy it regularly, they will think about which brands come to mind. These may not be the best brands, or even the brands that are most suitable for their needs, but they are the ones most available to memory.

Consumer implications

As mentioned in Chapter 2, it is very important for your brand to be 'mentally available', ie to easily come to mind when your consumers think of what options are available to them.

Hyperbolic discounting and emotional forecasting

Heuristic

Hyperbolic discounting is a fancy way of saying that people generally prefer rewards now rather than in the future. During most of our evolutionary history our ancestors were dependent upon uncertain food sources, so this preference for concrete resources now over possible resources in the future would have been very useful. Any promise of future food carried uncertainty. For example, most people would prefer a prize of £100 now over £120 in a month's time. This seems irrational when viewed from a purely logical and arithmetic perspective, but it is a good example of where a more ecological rationality is at work. In the real world, an offer of £120 in a month's time carries uncertainty: will the offer actually materialize? Can you trust the person making it?

Interestingly, our sensitivity to getting something sooner rather than later drops off over time. Differences between tomorrow and the day after will be greater than the difference between 100 days' time and 101 days' time, even though both involve a difference of one day.

Similarly, consumers are not always that good at remembering how they felt in the past, or predicting how they will feel in the future if they make certain spending choices. This is because of the 'peak–end' rule, mentioned in Chapter 2. We tend to remember experiences more by how we felt at the most intense moment and then at the end, rather than create a mental average of our feelings across the whole experience.

Consumer implications

How you leave consumers at the end of an experience – be it in-store, in a restaurant, or on a holiday – is disproportionately important to their memory of it, and hence their desire to experience it again.

Binary self-control and impulse purchases

Heuristic

Many religious rules may appear restrictive and hard for some to understand. For example, rules about complete abstinence from certain things (deemed to be unhealthy or undesirable to the community) or abstinence from those things on particular days of the year. This can seem arbitrary (why only on those days?) or just plain overly restrictive (why complete abstinence – can't we be allowed a little of the naughty food or drink in question?). However, these rules can look surprisingly similar to modern diets, such as the recently popular '5:2' diet in which adherents can eat freely for five days and then must eat only 25 per cent of their normal food intake for two days. Or no-carb diets in which people voluntarily choose to avoid any carbohydrate foods such as bread. People find it easier and simpler to totally abstain from something than to moderate their consumption of it. In contrast, when consumers are stressed or their conscious, rational brains have been working hard, they are more likely to abandon self-control and want to treat themselves.

Consumer implications

If you are promoting a healthy product or service, consider helping consumers kick their old bad habits by pointing out the benefits of total abstinence (or at least total abstinence for certain time periods). Or if you are promoting a treat or indulgent product or service, consider the times and places where people are most likely to be stressed or mentally tired.

Nudges: small interventions with big effects

Architect and designer Buckminster Fuller once said, 'I would never try to reform man – that's much too difficult. What I would do was to try to modify the environment in such a way as to get man moving in preferred directions.' Similarly, the applications of behavioural economics work on the principle that changing the environment – or at least the choices that consumers see presented to them – is often a more effective method than directly seeking to rationally persuade them of a choice.

A nudge (a term popularized in the 2008 book of the same name by Richard Thaler and Cass Sunstein) is essentially a way of using a heuristic to encourage people to behave in a certain way. A simple example of a consumer nudge is to place a product at eye-level height on the super-market shelves in order to increase its chance of being seen and therefore chosen. Nudges usually have a zen-like simplicity to them, and can be underestimated in their power as we tend to think that big effects require big efforts. Not so with nudges. They usually involve small changes, yet can create significant effects. The key thing with a nudge is that it should still retain people's freedom of choice, even if it tilts them in one direction.

Nudges have been used by both the US and British governments to influence positive behaviour, particularly in the area of health. During your average day as a consumer – seeing commercial messages and visiting the supermarket – the chances are that you have been nudged without realizing it!

CASE STUDY   Generosity at the restaurant Fifteen, Cornwall

Behavioural science specialists Mountainview (**www.mountainview.co.uk**) were asked by the UK Cabinet Office to help the restaurant Fifteen in Cornwall (a concept created by Jamie Oliver) to fund the training of apprentice chefs by 'encouraging' diners to the restaurant to make a donation.

Mountainview wanted to raise as much money as possible but not to do it at the expense of the morale of the staff (who may have lost tips) or the goodwill of the diners (who may have felt they were being taken advantage of).

Four experiments were devised, each testing a different heuristic route: 1) reframing the donation; 2) making the donation a default; 3) the use of reciprocity; 4) the use of social cues.

The result of the systematic testing was that Mountainview found that a £1 donation added to the bill by default (with the option to 'opt out') was most effective in terms of the interests of all stakeholders. Indeed this one simple 'nudge' managed to then raise around £100,000 in the coming year without any detrimental side effects to customer enjoyment or staff morale.

Mountainview's Thomas Bayne says, 'Developing behavioural interventions like this one can be very powerful, but they rest upon having a scientific and systematic approach in testing different possible nudges. They can be intimately dependent on the context and environment in which they are meant to work, and not all results in the lab or one context will translate successfully into another context.'[10]

Choice architecture and the $300 million button

Choice architecture is the process of structuring or framing options in such a way as to influence the likely outcome. It is particularly relevant to online retail, where often the ease of filling the shopping cart can make a large difference in sale volumes. Direct mail marketers have known this since the 1920s and often follow the rule of designing their print ads beginning with the coupon-form itself and working back from there. Whereas nudges are a general term to refer to any way in which behaviour can be encouraged via understanding the underlying heuristics that govern it, choice architecture refers more specifically to the moment when a choice or purchase is being made.

Usability writer Jared M Spool gives an example of how a badly designed e-commerce form was losing sales by annoying potential customers.[11] After customers had made their purchase on the site in question, they were prompted to either log into their account (assuming they had previously created one) or register to create a new one. Yet it was discovered that this familiar e-commerce request was actually putting off a lot of repeat customers (who often couldn't remember their log-in details) as well as first-time customers (who resented the feeling that they were being forced into a relationship with the supplier before they could make an order). A simple change was made to the form, replacing the 'register' button with one that simply said 'Continue', and underneath was a message telling shoppers that it wasn't necessary to register in order to make a purchase. This small change resulted in an additional $300 million in revenue during the coming year.

It may on the surface appear irrational, but relatively small things that are off-putting to potential customers can effectively be logjams that are holding back a hidden volume of extra sales.

Another interesting example of choice architecture was given by Dan Ariely, a professor in psychology and behavioural economics.[12] He describes a test conducted by the *Economist* magazine on their subscription options. Initially, would-be subscribers were presented with the following choices for formats:

Online: $59 (chosen by 68 per cent)

Print + Online: $125 (chosen by 32 per cent)

However, a third option was added, which shifted the response rates:

Online: $59 (chosen by 16 per cent)

Print + Online: $125 (chosen by 84 per cent)

Print: $125 (chosen by 0 per cent)

The simple addition of a print option at the same price as print + online shifted more people into spending a higher amount than in the first choice architecture (by being more likely to purchase the $125 print + online version). In the first instance, consumers have no easy way to assess how good a deal each option is, and it results in two-thirds choosing the cheaper option). However, in the second version there is now a pair of options in which one is obviously and dominantly better than the other, causing it to be overwhelmingly attractive. Just a simple change in the choice architecture communicates different values to consumers and can increase the overall expenditure they make.

Often choice architecture is not about actively persuading a consumer to make a choice, so much as removing barriers to them doing so. For example, risk-averse consumers often may want to buy a new untried product, or use an online retailer that they haven't used before, but may be prevented by fear of risk or inconvenience.

This is related to the principle of 'cognitive fluency' (discussed in Chapter 2) as it can be about making a process as smooth as possible, and require as little effortful thought as possible.

Another related technique is known as 'paving the cowpath'. This involves figuring out what consumers already naturally do, or want to do, and then clearing the path ahead of them (ie making the process as easy and cognitively smooth as possible). This will not only take advantage of the natural momentum of consumers, but will make the experience feel more cognitively fluent (see Chapter 3).

In Chapter 5 we look at ways of testing and discovering heuristics that your consumers may be using.

Summary

- Although consumers are constrained such that they cannot be fully rational, they are able to make choices that make rational sense within the contexts they live in.

- Value is often subjective, and consumers will tend to judge it more on relative comparisons than absolute amounts or costs.

- Consumers tend to satisfice: picking one or several product/ service features that they are not willing to compromise on, and others they are – arriving at a choice that is just good enough.

- Consumer choices are guided by mental biases or heuristics, which include a disproportionate fear of loss over opportunity of gain, and a tendency to be guided by quick – often non-conscious – emotional judgements about products and services.

- Nudges are minimalist interventions or changes that encourage consumers to act in a certain way. Choice architectures are the structures of choices that are presented to consumers. Changes in these – a type of nudge – can shift the heuristics that consumers are using, and change their choices.

Notes

1 McClure, SM, Li, J, Tomlin, D, Cypert, KS, Montague, M and Montague, PR (2004) Neural correlates of behavioral preference for culturally familiar drinks, *Neuron*, **44**, pp 379–87.

2 Plassmann, H, O'Doherty, J, Shiv, B and Rangel, A (2008) Marketing actions can modulate neural representations of experienced pleasantness, *PNAS*, **105** (3), pp 1050–54.

3 Hsee, CK (1998) Less is better: when low-value options are valued more highly than high-value options, *Journal of Behavioral Decision Making*, **11**, pp 107–21.

4 Tversky, A and Kahneman, D (1974) Judgment under uncertainty: heuristics and biases, *Science*, **185**, pp 1124–30.

5 Ariely, D (2008) *Predictably Irrational*, Harpercollins, London.

6 Sutherland, S (1992) *Irrationality*, Pinter and Martin, London.

7 Lindgaard, G, Fernandes, G, Dudek, C and Brown, J (2006) Attention web designers: you have 50 milliseconds to make a good first impression!, *Behaviour and Information Technology*, **25** (2), pp 115–26.

8 Ambady, N and Rosenthal, R (1993) Half a minute: predicting teacher evaluations from thin slices of nonverbal behaviour and physical attractiveness, *Journal of Personality and Social Psychology*, **64** (3), pp 431–41.

9 For details on the mixed results achieved with this kind of 'social proof' nudge, see: Schultz, P, Nolan, JM, Cialdini, RB, Goldstein, NJ and

Griskevicius, V (2007) The constructive, destructive, and reconstructive power of social norms, *Psychological Science*, **18** (5), pp 429–34. In some cases there was what the authors call a 'boomerang' effect: by informing people of the norm amongst their peers, if people are actually on the right side of the norm, they may gravitate towards it (eg college students who drink less than average, when told of average alcohol consumption may drink more). However, by adding a smiling or frowning emoticon to the information about their relationship to the norms (showing approval if they were below, disapproval above) the researchers found they could stop this boomerang effect.

10 Personal communication with the author.

11 Spool, J [accessed 24 April 2015] The $300 Million Button, *User Interface Engineering* [Online] http://www.uie.com/articles/three_hund_million_button/.

12 Ariely, D (2012) *The (Honest) Truth About Dishonesty*, HarperTorch, New York.

PART TWO
THE NEW RESEARCH TOOLS

GUIDELINES FOR EXPERIMENTS

05

In the previous three chapters we looked at a number of mental biases and insights that can explain consumer reactions that would traditionally be deemed irrational or at least non-conscious. These theoretical findings can be a useful preparation for running and interpreting studies. At the beginning they can help form hypotheses for designing studies to test, and afterwards they can help explain test results. As a generality, the biases and neuro-principles described in Chapters 2 and 3 are most relevant to questions about design, and the sensory (including visual) appeal of ads and communications. The biases covered in Chapter 4 are more relevant to questions about prices, perceived value, and how consumers make comparative choices or fill in online shopping carts. The remainder of the book describes the new methodologies for testing creative material. Before we examine each technique there are some general principles for running experiments. If you have a science degree or strong science background you are at an advantage here. If not, this chapter will help orient you (Table 5.1).

TABLE 5.1   A summary of the ways that theories and practices relate to each other

	Media/Communications Effectiveness	Values, Prices and Choices
Theory	Neuro-biases Neuroaesthetics (ie Chapter 3)	Heuristics (ie Chapter 4)
Research	Neuro-research (eg implicit response measures, eye-tracking, facial action coding)	A versus B testing of nudges or changes to choice architectures

One of the first things to note is that these types of test work by presenting people with stimuli or choices and getting their reactions. They do not work by asking consumers to create ideas, or come up with responses to things you haven't exposed them to. You can get their reactions to several executions for ideas for your new ad, but you cannot get them to reveal what their theoretical, ultimate ideal ad would be. These tests are fundamentally reactive. Also, they are not suited to testing large volumes of material at once, as participants tire and cannot be expected to give repeatedly fresh reactions if you keep them too long.

There are always limits on how much stimuli you can show to participants. For one thing, people become fatigued if the tests run on too long. However, there are also considerations around the content of the stimulus itself. If the different designs or ads are too similar then you may need to run them in different testing cells of people, so that each person does not see them all. Humans are not just reactive machines that you put material in front of and they give you the same reaction each time. Rather they will often seek patterns in what you are showing them. If you repeatedly show them very similar materials they will begin to actively search for the differences between them, or just habituate and become less attentive. Either way, you will be disrupting the more natural consumer response.

However, within these restrictions there is still a large scope for things to investigate. It also means that, ultimately, the creative power is still with the designers, copywriters and sundry creatives who devise your communications to begin with. They will already have their own intuitions about what works and what doesn't; this is just an extra source of either confirmation of these, or additional insights to enrich their body of understanding.

One of the more typical types of tests is often referred to as a 'beauty contest': the comparison of several possible variants of, for example, a design of an ad, or concepts for a campaign or product. By testing them against each other before launching, spending can be optimized by choosing the one that is most likely to engage consumers, or most likely to meet the brief for the aims of the communication. Equally, these tests can act as a kind of safety net, which can help reveal any weaknesses in a communication before it is launched.

Principles for neuro-testing

In the early 20th century it seemed probable that airships – craft connected to giant oval-shaped balloons filled with lighter-than-air gas – would become the primary means of intercontinental passenger transport.[1] Their size and majesty impressed and they ran regular routes across the Atlantic. In contrast, airplanes were small, inexpensive and lacked such prestige. However, it was their very size and cheapness that spurred their fast development: they were within the reach of more people, to create and tinker with; in a word, to experiment. This meant that a lot was learned about them in a relatively short time and they evolved into the safest form of transport that we have now. Similarly, most of the methods covered in this book, whilst perhaps not having the glamour of the brain-scanning technologies, are more amenable to fast, cheap testing. Therefore, they will likely continue to be adopted by market researchers, and the body of knowledge coming from them will continue to build.

This ideal – of fast, cheap testing – is important, I believe, to how one approaches researching the irrational consumer. The best practice for running research studies in this area can be summarized as follows:

1 Clearly define your research question. This includes thinking about what type of information you would need to answer the question, which will help you pick the most suitable methodology (more on this in the individual chapters on each methodology).

2 Form a hypothesis about how you expect the results to turn out, and why.

3 Analyse the results of the study in the light of your hypothesis and, again, use neuro-principles to interpret your results.

4 If necessary, test your conclusions by repeating steps one to three.

Without this loop of 'hypothesis – test – refine hypotheses – retest' you can sometimes end up with inconclusive results: you may think you have found a new principle that is driving your consumers, but you can't be sure. However, whilst retesting can be a virtue, sometimes it can also be useful to do one-off tests to gain quick feedback on things like choosing between several design executions, or even just to test that a route you plan to go with doesn't have any serious problems. In either case, research techniques that you can operate comparatively more cheaply or quickly will usually have the edge over more elaborate and expensive ones.

We will now look at some of the other important principles to bear in mind when planning experiments.

Realism versus control

One of the most frequent research requests from clients is for testing in real-world environments; ideally to expose consumers to their stimuli in situ (eg in a real supermarket setting). Whilst this is often technically possible (eg with eye-tracking studies, you can use mobile eye-trackers and send people around a real store, measuring what they look at), it is often practically difficult. The reason is that if you do not control what your test participants are exposed to, on a second-by-second basis, then you will find it much harder to aggregate your results, and analysis becomes a time-consuming 'by hand' effort. For example, you could send off a group of people into even just one supermarket aisle, wearing portable eye-trackers (which is possible as they are now as small as large spectacles), in order to study where shoppers are looking, and if they look at your product etc. However, even within the constraints of allowing them to just explore one aisle, each shopper will have their heads orientated at different angles, at different fields of view second by second. This is fine if you have sophisticated software for 'tagging' visual zones of interest, but if not, the data analysis will have to be aggregated 'by hand', which is time-consuming. In contrast, if you show all study participants either a series of still images (photos, or computer renderings, for example) of the supermarket aisle, or a video depicting a shopper point-of-view journey down the aisle, you now have enough commonality between them to aggregate the results.

Some marketers worry that showing videos or still images will not be realistic enough. However, if you are merely trying to get a comparative reaction between several executions, then it is not quite so much of a concern. It is more of a consideration if you believe that consumers genuinely will not understand what it is that you are showing them. If so, you can provide a brief explanation at the beginning of the study (eg 'you are about to see a range of new pack designs for a premium chocolate product'). This can usually be done with a line or two of on-screen text.

This type of testing is a little more akin to running a scientific study than a typical market research project. In neuro-research we are measuring subtle responses to stimuli, so we need to make efforts to minimize other possible influences on participants' reactions. This means that the testing needs to be disciplined by: 1) making efforts to ensure that all participants go through exactly the same experience; 2) making sure that there are no other influences on participants' reactions – for example, that none of the participants are given any extra information beforehand about the content of the study.

Lastly, an important consideration when selecting your stimuli to test is the level of quality and similarity between each stimulus. Obviously, it will be an unfair and meaningless test to compare a finished ad against one that is still a sketch or animatic. When testing a bunch of materials, they should all be of comparable quality of finish.

Recruitment and cultural differences

Another question that researchers new to non-conscious measures often ask is who they need to recruit for studies. For example, if they do a study with participants recruited from one population, will the results be generalizable to others?

The good news is that the considerations with your sample recruitment are broadly the same as with traditional market research. You need to define your target market of consumers and work out questions that will help recruit them. For a behavioural study it may be as simple as just letting the test run amongst your regular customers. If you need to recruit participants, then they can be recruited in the same way that you would with traditional research (eg through specialist recruitment companies, or through advertising).

The considerations over how much you can generalize the results of your study are also largely the same as with traditional research. If you think that the material you are testing is likely to be interpreted differently in different countries or cultures then you either need to run separate tests amongst them or generalize only with great care. Usually the metrics themselves do not change between cultures, but the way that people will interpret the meaning and content can. For example, if people in the United States and Japan genuinely find an ad to be amusing, the metrics can pick this up, but the *types* of ads or content that make people find something amusing in those two cultures can, obviously, be different. The cultural meanings attached to the stimuli you use are influenced by the histories and assumptions of those cultures.

Benchmarking and normalizing

If you are lucky enough to have access to a database of previous results from your method of choice, then you may be able to either normalize the data you get, or compare it to the typical mean and range. This can be useful to tell how reactions to your stimuli have compared to previous reactions, but a couple of caveats should be borne in mind. First, the database should be composed of reactions to the same media. For example, video is generally more stimulating (ie attention-grabbing, and often emotionally engaging) than a still image, therefore it wouldn't be meaningful to compare reactions to a cereal packet design with a database of highly emotionally engaging cinema ads. Second, you may want to consider the composition of the database in terms of the content of the stimuli tested that made it up (for example, was it from stimuli from the same industry sector as your own? If not, is it sensible to compare them?) and the testing populations that made it up (were they comparable to your own testing population?), although this latter consideration is somewhat less important as long as each population was appropriate to the content it was testing. Third, it may sometimes be important to check that the database is composed of recordings from the same or similar experimental design as your current test. The way that a study design is constructed may itself affect the range of results, and hence be a relevant consideration in comparisons.

A key distinction is between benchmarked databases and databases that are simply normalized sets of data. Any set of results can have its distribution plotted, but this does not necessarily tell you anything about the real-world performance of the ads that scored at each position along the curve. For example, all the data in the database may have come from above-average-performing ads, in which case any comparison with it will be skewed in that direction. In contrast, a benchmarked database will have comparisons with an independent performance variable, such as real-world marketplace performance, and will therefore be more informative about the likely competitive performance of the ad.

In the beginning stages, if you are using a third-party vendor to provide the testing tech, they will often have their own databases and will be able to guide you on normalizing or benchmarking the data. If you don't have this luxury, you may just need to treat the results purely as comparisons between the stimuli at hand.

Another approach can be to use a 'control' stimulus in your test, perhaps one that you already know the performance of, or understand well, as a point of comparison.

Lab, online and real-world testing

Another consideration is the context in which you run your study. As mentioned, there are virtues in having tighter levels of control than a naturalistic study. With behavioural economics-style testing this is not so much of a concern, as these can be run 'live' in real-world contexts, but with testing things such as packaging or point-of-sale communications you need to decide between testing in a lab, online or in the real world. In most cases it will not make sense to test in real-world environments as it is just not practical or necessary. For example, imagine if you have some in-store point-of-sale posters to test. In order to test them in situ there are considerable cost and time considerations in getting all your participants to the location, as well as potential 'noise' in the data from having different combinations of other shoppers, sound etc, affecting their experiences. Also, operating most of the technologies described in this book in a real-world environment is far more challenging than in a controlled environment.

This leaves 'lab' versus online. Several of the techniques covered in later chapters can be used online. Participants can be recruited from online panels, then after qualification via a screening questionnaire they will be directed to a link for the test. As completing such a test from your home computer is usually relatively quick and convenient, payment levels are typically lower, therefore studies conducted online are cheaper. They also have the benefit of being relatively quick to set up, and can be run anywhere in the world where you can find an online recruiter and penetration of computers that is high enough to make it feasible.

A neuro-testing lab can simply mean any sufficiently quiet space with good lighting/heating control, and that is a convenient place to which participants can travel. It could be a dedicated lab, or it might just be a typical office room, or even a hired conference room in a hotel. The benefits of a lab-type environment are that you have somewhat more control over the testing. You can see if participants are focused on the test and are completing it correctly. You can answer any of their questions in person, and you can control the way that they see the stimuli (for example, ensuring everyone sees the images or video on exactly the same size screen, from the same distance away from the screen etc). The drawback compared to online is that it is more expensive. Not only might you need to rent or buy a testing location, but it is less convenient for participants to have to travel to a location, therefore you need to pay them more.

Interesting questions for experiments

Given below are some examples of questions that each type of study can be good at answering.

Behavioural economics and nudging

Behavioural economics ideas are ideal for testing as they are all about behaviour (and hence do not suffer from the challenges of asking people questions). Equally, whereas creating new executions of ads or designs for testing can be expensive and time-consuming, the materials for testing nudges or changes to choice architectures are usually far simpler and quicker to prepare:

- Which way of wording a price reduction is most attractive to consumers?
- Which features of a product or service are having the most influence on consumers and on which are they willing to compromise?
- Does your current typical consumer ordering or purchasing path have any pain points? What would be the effect of removing or lessening these?
- What apparently irrational worries or fears might consumers have about purchasing from you? How can you neutralize these?
- Does offering a different range of choices shift the average spend across a whole category? Or change how consumers value the other options on offer?

Behavioural economics ideas are usually most suitable to testing at the point of purchase: in-store or on an e-commerce site. A typical test might involve experimenting with your online ordering. Of course, the notion of changing store displays or order forms is not in itself a radical or new idea. However, it is the ideas from behavioural economics themselves that open our minds to new possibilities that a more rational consumer model would not even consider.

Devising nudges themselves can be a bit of an art and can require some creative or at least lateral thinking. Just reading about a previously successful nudge can be a little like discovering how a magic trick was done: interesting but not always enough information to devise your own. Nevertheless, you can model your own nudges based on past examples, adapted to your own circumstances. The first step would be to look through the list of heuristics in Chapter 4 (and other heuristics can easily be found online or in the recommended reading list) and ask yourself which might be in effect in your commercial situation.

Another way of generating ideas for nudges comes from a form of therapy called 'solution-focused brief therapy'. This practical technique assumes that the solution to someone's problem can already exist if only it can be found in the person's existing everyday behaviour. Very few problems exist continually, 24/7, and therefore by identifying the moments when the problem is not present you can often identify the factors that will provide a solution. By applying this way of thinking to nudging consumers we can ask the question: when do consumers already happily do the behaviour you would like them to? This is a different way of thinking from the typical alternatives such as: 1) what we might call the engineer mindset – where problems are solved by making significant material alterations (usually at great cost) to either the product environment or the service; 2) the coercive mindset, where you try to directly force people to act in a particular way – again, usually at higher cost than a nudge (by, for example, discounting prices, or by risking alienating consumers by forcing them into a particular action).

Table 5.2 gives some examples that show the contrast between these ways of thinking, and how the solutions-focused philosophy can suggest a nudge. Notice also that none of the nudge ideas shown in Table 5.2 feel like a sting, chaff or push to the consumer (as some of the solutions from the other mindsets might) so much as inviting them to behave in ways that they are already comfortable with.

When you come to plan a study (or want to double-check the plans of your supplier) the checklist given here lists some useful things to remember.

TABLE 5.2   Engineering and coercive versus nudge solutions

Commercial Problem	Engineering Mindset Solution	Coercive Mindset Solution	Nudge
Increase the average spend on subscriptions to your magazine.	Get your subscription ads out into more places (eg more leaflets in magazine or in-store). Perhaps effective but at a cost.	Reduce the choice options to only the more expensive choices (eg only offer 12 months rather than 6, or 18 rather than 12).	Consumers are happy to pay more if they see a choice as a bargain in comparison to another choice presented at the same time (see the *Economist* example in Chapter 4). (Also, given that consumers value immediate over future gratification, consider allowing them to pick up their first copy immediately from a shop.)
Customers waiting in queues – either on the phone or in stores or restaurants – get bored and are sometimes liable to abandon the queue, resulting in either lost business or unhappy customers.	Open more checkouts or pay for more staff to answer your phones or wait tables in your restaurant.	Try schemes to speed up your staff's interaction with customers so that they spend less time per customer and the queues move faster (albeit risking a lower-quality experience per customer), or warn customers that they may experience a long waiting time.	A simple insight: we are less likely to feel bored or frustrated when we have something to distract us. Give waiting customers something to think about, such as information they would find useful, and they are less likely to abandon the queue.[2]

Continues overleaf

TABLE 5.2 *continued*

Commercial Problem	Engineering Mindset Solution	Coercive Mindset Solution	Nudge
The train journey time between London and Paris is deemed to be too long and hence inconvenient to travellers.	Put in a high-speed rail connection (this was the actual solution adopted in the UK, costing £5.8 billion).	Warn consumers by drawing attention to the journey time and remind them to build it into their plans.	The engineering solution fails to consider that the total journey time is also comprised of waiting around in the railway stations. By creating a simple smartphone app that allows passengers to jump on an earlier available train if they happen to arrive early could just as easily shorten total journey lengths for many at much lower cost.[3]
Sugary food products harm children's (and adults'!) teeth. A problem that parents are increasingly aware of, and hence may make them think of boycotting sugary treat foods for their children.	Reduce the sugar content of the product (perhaps at risk of ruining or weakening the taste and pleasure of eating it).	Ban the advertising of sugary foods or seek to find ways to minimize the amounts that children are allowed to eat.	When might the effect of sugar naturally be lessened? When the child brushes their teeth afterwards. And when might they be amenable to doing so? If they were given a reminder that was fun and seemingly a natural part of the experience. Colgate gave away free ice-cream lollies. When the ice cream is eaten it reveals that the stick is actually in the shape of a toothbrush and says 'Don't forget Colgate'.[4]

Checklist

Behaviour-nudging tests

☐ Have all other possible relevant influences on consumer choices been kept the same whilst you make your test of different options?

☐ Is the context of your test the same as that of the situation in which you hope to eventually implement it?

☐ Consider the full range of contextual details in which your nudge will exist in the real world. For example, what other options will be available to consumers (and hence be compared to yours)?

☐ Could your nudge be seen by consumers as overly manipulative, tricksy or encouraging choices that are bad for them or their children? Such nudges can easily backfire and damage a company's reputation, given the power that consumers now have to communicate their displeasure not only through word of mouth but in online reviews and social media.

People are not predictable in a push-button way, the way that a Newtonian mechanical machine would be. Indeed, we may have evolved to have unpredictability built into our behaviour and thinking, to make us less easy to control or manipulate! So testing nudges rigorously in their natural real-world context is essential.

Neuroaesthetics and neuro-design principles

Here are some examples for testing reactions to the appeals of various forms of designs and commercial communications:

- Which of several executions of a package or print ad design or a video ad is better? Which best evokes the concepts and emotions of the design/ad brief?

- Which elements of a design or ad work best, and which could be improved (and how)?

- Is a package being seen on-shelf? And, if so, how long does it take for shoppers to see it?

Checklist

Neuro-tests

☐ Don't show the same participants too many very similar executions of a stimulus, lest you bore them or force them into an artificial 'spot the difference' game.

☐ Ensure that all your stimuli are of a comparable quality of 'finish' so that you are not unwittingly biasing responses on the basis of quality rather than content.

☐ Think carefully about the wording of any instructions and description before participants see the stimuli, so as not to overly bias or prime their reactions.

☐ Have you made sure that the order in which participants will see your stimuli has been controlled for, to ensure that none of the stimuli are being unfairly biased by the order in which they are seen?

☐ Ensure that your participants are qualified to be able to undertake the study. Make sure they have good-enough eyesight to see your images or videos, that they will be able to read on-screen instructions, and have good-enough understanding of the language you are using. If the test is online, you may need to check that their computer equipment matches the minimum standards and falls within the range of variance of equipment that you are willing to accept (eg screen sizes).

Summary

- Neuro-testing works by displaying stimuli to people and getting their reactions. It needs to be treated more like a scientific experiment than traditional market research.

- Fast and (comparatively) cheap can be virtues of these types of tests as they allow for a greater volume of testing, and hence the ability to check hypotheses.

- Whilst marketers instinctively want 'realism' in the testing set-up, keeping tests screen-based offers a level of control that is needed for these types of tests.

- Considerations for recruiting study participants are largely the same as for traditional research.

- There are pros and cons for testing in a central location/lab versus online.

- Normative databases can provide a useful means of assessing your test results but may not always be available. Other forms of comparison are also possible.

Notes

1 This example appears in: Dyson, F (1997) *Imagined Worlds*, Harvard University Press, London.

2 This idea comes from: Janakiraman, N, Meyer, RJ and Hoch, SJ (2011) The psychology of decisions to abandon waits for service, *Journal of Marketing Research*, **48** (6), pp 970–84.

3 I am indebted to Rory Sutherland, vice chairman of Ogilvy and Mather UK, for this ingenious idea.

4 AODW [accessed 24 April 2015] Colgate: Don't forget, Ice-cream [Online] http://adsoftheworld.com/media/dm/colgate_don_t_forget_icecream.

EYE-TRACKING 06

In the early 1970s Hollywood film editor Walter Murch made an interesting discovery – whilst editing *The Conversation* (1974) he noticed that the star, Gene Hackman, tended to blink around the moment when he made a cut.[1] The natural point at which to edit the scenes was somehow also being non-consciously perceived by the actor and being expressed by a blink. Rather than being just a mechanical means to moisten the eye, it seemed that blinking was a means for the person to separate out thoughts and perceptions, meaning that the natural point where one shot would end would be felt by the actor. Murch believes that if you could track the eyes of an entire cinema audience, a deeply immersive film that engaged them would reveal hundreds of eyes blinking in unison in the dark, in non-conscious sympathy with the screen.

Whilst no one has yet tested this idea, tracking people's eye movement activity is possible, even in the dark. If you shine an infrared light on someone's eyes, they can't see it, but their eyes reflect the light back, which can then be picked up by an infrared camera (the effect looks like the 'red eye' that sometimes appears in photos). This is the mechanism behind many of today's market research and usability eye-trackers.

We live in a visual culture, with more information delivered via our eyes than any other sense. Whilst we live in a particularly cluttered visual environment today, making images has probably been a human preoccupation for at least tens of millennia, as the cave paintings on the Indonesian island of Sulawesi and Ardèche in the south of France dramatically illustrate (the paintings here are at least 35,000 years old). Some were even designed to animate when viewed under flickering firelight. Unsurprisingly, half the brain is dedicated to processing what we see. Yet today we are perhaps more visually sophisticated than ever, having got used to rapidly extracting visual information from fast-cut TV, quick web-page browsing, and flicking through magazines and newspapers. This means that our eyes move quickly from one thing to another, and we are ever more selective about what we give our attention to. Our thinking and our choices are probably dominated more by what we are currently looking at than anything else.

How we see

Hundreds of millions of years of evolution have crafted for us a visual system that is extremely efficient at allowing us to build a high-definition view of our surroundings with a minimal amount of information-bandwidth. Yet what we see is not akin to a photograph taken by the camera of our eyes, but a constructed image based on a visual search coupled with our memory for things we have seen before. This process is real, but non-conscious and unintuitive.

Whilst we have already seen how the energy expended when we use system 2 thinking makes us cognitive misers, we are also stingy with our attention due to information overload. As such, there is a double challenge for anyone wishing to deliver information visually: standing out against all the visual clutter whilst also winning attention with consumers who are highly selective about what they look at.

Our intuitive experience tells us that we view the world around us in one go, but we don't. Instead we have a tiny area of focused vision that we move around in rapid jumps, then our brain fills in the gaps. For example, you may believe that you can smoothly move your eyes across the view in front of you, but you can't. Ask someone else to try this; as you watch their eyes you will see that they actually make a series of small, fast (between one-hundredth and one-tenth of a second) jumps, called saccades. When our eyes perform a saccadic movement the image received by the retina is blurred, meaning that we are essentially blind during these visual leaps, although, of course, we have no conscious awareness of this!

Now slowly move your finger from one side to the other and ask someone to follow it with their gaze. This time you will find that they can. This is called a smooth pursuit, and it is an eye movement that we can only perform when we have a moving target to guide us.

The illusion of a seamless, detailed and colourful visual scene is only possible due to the almost constant movement of our eyes. We may intuitively feel that we can shift our attention around this scene at will in order to examine details, but this is also an illusion. If we want to shift our attention, we almost always need to shift our eyes.

Light enters through the cornea and the lens of our eyes, which can become more curved or flat depending on its focusing on closer or more distant objects. It hits the retina, where there are around 120 million rod cells (the most sensitive, but which don't work in colour) and around 6–7 million cone cells (providing colour vision). The pupil can become larger or smaller depending on light conditions, but also on the person's emotional interest and cognitive load. In practice this measure, called pupillometry, is often measured by an eye-tracking camera, but I have included more about it in Chapter 9 on biometrics.

Detail versus gist

The fovea is the part of the retina that is most sensitive and provides our fine detailed vision, but only covers an area equivalent in size to your thumbnail at arm's length (approximately three degrees of our visual field) – shockingly small! This is the region that eye-trackers measure. Surrounding our region of foveal vision is our peripheral vision. The further out from the central foveal position something is, the weaker the visual acuity we have. Our peripheral vision provides more coarse, less coloured information, yet is good at detecting movement.

Whilst we only have the ability to scrutinize in detail what is within our foveal vision, we also have some awareness of what is surrounding it in the peripheral zones. It is this awareness that helps drive where we next focus; if something in our peripheral view looks interesting, or is important to decoding what is in front of us, our eyes move to meet it. The more well known an image is to us, and the simpler it is, the more likely our peripheral vision will recognize it.

If we don't fixate on something we may still recognize it. If we see it a lot in our peripheral vision it may still be going into our memory and hence becoming more familiar to us. Similarly, if we only fixate on something very briefly, it is the overall gist or gestalt of the image that we are likely to see.

Taken together, these two facts about how we see underlie the importance of making key design elements, such as logos and packaging, distinctive and easy to perceive. This not only helps consumers to find your product if they are looking for it amongst the visual clutter of a supermarket, shop, website or print publication, but also helps them to recognize it regularly, whenever it appears peripherally or fleetingly in vision, making it more familiar.

One thing that is not yet fully understood is the degree to which things that we see regularly or repetitively in our peripheral vision, or things that we only fixate on briefly, may be influencing us over the longer term. For example, the more we see a logo in our peripheral vision, the more familiar it is likely to feel to us; and thanks to the familiarity heuristic (see Chapter 3) this could create a bias towards us choosing that brand when we are next standing in front of the supermarket shelves. There is some evidence for this. For example, one study demonstrated that web-banner ads for fictitious brands that were not directly focused on were still able to have a non-conscious effect: viewers were subsequently more likely to consider choosing that brand, even though they could not consciously recall having seen the ad.[2] Interestingly, the study also found that whilst animated banner ads were generally no better than static ones at this incidental priming effect, they were more effective when they were placed in similar or congruent web-page content. These results show that just evaluating web-banner ads on eye-tracking fixations, click-throughs or conscious recall may blind researchers to the longer-term implicit brand-building potential. The more we are incidentally exposed to a brand, the more familiar it becomes and the more likely we are to consider it.

This highlights the importance of brands, ads and visual communications to be clear and distinctive. They should be able to communicate the brand even if seen unclearly, very briefly or from the corner of our eye. At this level of gestalt, or gist, distinctive colours and shapes are of particular importance. The bright-red swirly Coca-Cola logo, or the dynamic Nike tick-swoosh, are good examples of imagery that is distinctive and simple enough that we are likely to easily process it non-consciously in our periphery.

Eye-trackers

Amazingly, the first eye-trackers were made in the late 1800s, but they were mechanical and required a small ring actually attached to the eyeball. In the early to mid-20th century, researchers began building non-invasive eye-trackers but it was not until the mid-1970s that they began to be manufactured so that you could buy them 'off the shelf'. There are now several big manufacturers.

Eye-tracking (ET) can require the least sophistication of experimental design and statistical analysis. Most ET software can perform automatic analyses of your data, meaning that you only need to get involved with the more complex statistical side of ET analysis if you have more complex research requirements.

Questions that eye-tracking is good at addressing include:

- Does a package 'pop out' on the shelf – ie when someone is freely looking at a shelf display, does your package stand out?
- Is a package easily locatable on the shelf – ie when consumers are asked specifically to search for it, how long does it take? More usefully, what are the varying lengths of time taken to find alternative pack designs?

- Given a very short viewing time, what do people see – ie what are the first things they look at? This is particularly pertinent as in many instances people will only look at an ad for a fraction of a second.

- What does a typical person's visual search of a particular web page look like? How easy to use is the site and how easy is it for people to find what they want?

- Which regions of a given print publication or website tend to get looked at most and least? (And, hence, where is the most valuable 'real estate' for advertisers?)

- On a package design, do the typical fixations and scan paths suggest that people are easily able to extract the critical fragments of information, or is attention dispersed across the pack, with large distances between fixations and no central focus of attention? (The latter suggests that people may have to mentally work harder to decode the design, making it less effective.)

- Is the brand information clearly visible?

- Does the pack work well with both those who are loyalists and those who will be making up their minds whilst in-store?

There are many types of outputs that can be generated from eye-tracking data, but the most frequently used in advertising/marketing studies is the heat map (see Figure 6.1). Two other important terms are fixations and saccades/scan path. A fixation is when the eyes rest on a particular point and begin to take in detailed information. A scan path is the pattern of where the person fixated (this often is useful as it shows the order of which elements of an image a person looked at). There are numerous other measurements that can be calculated, and different ways of calculating and displaying these, but the two mentioned above are the most frequently used in market research.

Results can then be visualized in a number of ways:

- *Heat maps*: these are coloured regions overlaid on an image that resemble clouds of attention, and currently seem to be the most frequently offered eye-tracking output. Whilst the heat map in Figure 6.1 is shown in greyscale, the maps are usually colour-coded so that the warmer the colour the higher the levels of attention to that area (eg red shows the highest amounts of attention, blue the lowest). Heat maps can be computed either based on the number of fixations or total gaze duration on an area, or on the number of people who looked at the area. The difference between the two can affect how one interprets the results, so it is important to be clear on how your system is calculating this.

● *Gaze plots*: these show the typical pattern of the order of fixations on the image or video. This can be calculated for an individual (called a gaze replay) or group (called a bee swarm).

FIGURE 6.1   A heat map (left) and gaze plot (right) for a tea-packaging label

Eye-tracking data for still images are somewhat easier to interpret than for video. The typical output for a video is in a video dashboard where the overall attention for the group is illustrated with an overlaid bee swarm (a series of moving dots, each representing the eye movements of an individual person) or a moving heat map.

For these types of outputs, interpretation tends to be qualitative, by simply looking at the videos and drawing conclusions, although more numerical or statistical analyses are possible if you can set up defined areas of interest within the video. Nevertheless, even 'by eye' you can quickly answer questions such as whether most people saw key elements within the ad, such as branding or key bits of information. It can be easier to interpret these video visualizations when viewed in slow motion.

ET apparently gives intuitively clear, unambiguous data: it shows where someone's eyes moved, and is not subject to black-box algorithms to get to that data. In theory you could have carefully observed the person's eyes yourself to have confirmed the results. However, in practice, the outputs that you will use are all subject to calculations, and it is important to understand exactly what each one is showing when you interpret it. Equally, there is always an element of ambiguity in eye-tracking data if used on its own. It shows us where the person was looking but not what their thoughts or feelings were when they looked at something. We can only infer this information, or obtain it from additional measures.

There are three main eye-tracking technologies that are used by market researchers:

- *Lab-based eye-tracking*: infrared light is shone onto the person's eyes and is reflected back from the front of the cornea and the back of the lens (these are called Purkinje reflections). The relationship of the cornea's reflection to the fovea is not so affected by head movements, only eye rotation. Yet this can be compensated for with a calibration task and some calculations done automatically in the background.

  Such trackers typically make up to 50 or 60 measurements per second, with a spatial resolution of around half a degree, which is more than adequate for most marketing questions. The data is essentially just a series of X/Y co-ordinates and time codes to link to the presentation of stimuli, so that the co-ordinates can later be overlaid on whatever video or image was being presented on-screen.

- *Online eye-tracking*: as with implicit response measures, the proliferation of computers with high-speed internet connections as well as high-definition webcams means that eye-tracking studies can now be conducted online. The benefit of this is that studies can be conducted more cheaply and often faster. Critics claim that the quality of online recordings is not yet good enough, with the data not providing a high-enough level of precision due to the lack of a controlled environment for testing, and the use of just one webcam. However, with improvements in technology and software power, it is likely that these criticisms will carry less weight over time.

  In addition to eye movements, online eye-tracking can potentially also incorporate other measures, such as facial action coding (automated measures of facial emotional expressions; see Chapter 8), changes in facial skin colour that show changes in heart rate and posture movements that can indicate interest.

- *Mobile eye-tracking*: mobile eye-trackers are available that are just like a large pair of spectacles. The benefit of these is that they allow recording whilst a person is in a real-world environment, such as browsing in a supermarket. The main drawback is that the data is a lot more time intensive to interpret, as each person will have had, moment by moment, a different and unique field of view.

  Mobile eye-trackers really come into their own with research questions that combine the need to understand real-world shopper navigation with gaze directions. For example, when shoppers walk around a supermarket, where do they go? In what order? Where do they choose to stop? And how do their patterns of gaze correlate with these behaviours? Was it a particular sign, or pack design, that grabbed their attention and attracted them to move in closer? Does the order in which they see signs or other point of sale material affect what they subsequently look at? Sometimes these questions can also be tackled with a screen-based virtual-reality simulation, where the participants have a video-game-like ability to control the movement around a virtual store. However, it is not yet fully understood how lifelike behaviours are in such virtual environments, and they are also costly to create. Sometimes even glasses that just have a tiny camera in their bridge can be useful for studying shopper behaviour. These are not true eye-trackers but will capture the general field of view.

Mouse-tracking is a simpler and cheaper alternative to eye-tracking. Researchers have found some correlation between where a person looks and where they move a mouse cursor. When used on website studies it can be indicative of where a person is moving their attention or where they might have considered clicking but didn't (although it obviously suffers from the limitations that some people simply only move their mouse when they are definitely about to click, or to scroll the page up or down). A variant of mouse-tracking that is more useful for still images (such as print ads, posters or package images) involves shading out the whole screen except for a visible halo around the cursor, obliging the participant to move the cursor to whichever regions they want to see. This method is, however, impractical for web studies (as the mouse needs to be used in different ways), too slow for videos, and does not usually work well on in-store images (it can result in the participants adopting an unnatural scanning path across each shelf, one by one).

A typical eye-tracking study is very non-intrusive from a participant perspective. Other than a mobile eye-tracker study, the participant will usually sit in front of a screen and first go through a calibration procedure. This would typically be a dot, number or crosshair that will move into set positions on the screen, which they are instructed to follow using their eyes only (ie not moving their head). This allows the software to then understand which positions of eye movement of the person correspond to which regions of the screen. From there onwards there is minimum experimental fuss, with the person simply being asked to view the images or videos. The eye-tracking recording requires nothing extra from them, although such studies are typically also combined with other measures.

What draws the eye?

Our gaze is simultaneously driven by top-down and bottom-up factors. Top-down factors loosely map on to conscious, system 2 thinking and include your goals or motivations for looking at something. For example, we are very good at ignoring ads that we don't want to see. In general, if we deem something to have low personal relevance, we will not look at it. For example, if you cannot afford a luxury new car you are likely to avoid gazing at the print ads for them. However, if something makes it relevant, such as the inclusion of your favourite actor or actress in the image, you are more likely to look. Equally, if we are searching for something, our visual scanning will obviously be influenced by our search for it.

When we read a page of text there are, obviously, predictable scan paths (from top to bottom, left to right in English), but there is no universal scan path for viewing an image. Nevertheless, given the same image, there will be commonalities between people in the way they scan it, yet these can differ depending on the person's search goals. When we look at something we may allow our eyes to be drawn just to whatever looks most interesting, or what requires the most focus to understand (eg if something is visually complex or novel), or we may be more actively searching for information. Therefore, either bottom-up features of an image or top-down search goals can influence a scan path when looking at an image.

Nevertheless, some common eye-tracking features have been discovered. These differ according to media type. For example, a typical person browsing the web will adopt a far faster scanning/browsing pattern of viewing than when they are reading a magazine. In a magazine or newspaper, the ads will be in a competitive environment (competing for attention with other ads) to a degree that billboards, for example, don't suffer. Understanding the different behavioural contexts, goals and typical scan paths of different media can be helpful in identifying the most valuable places to position your ad.

Whilst an exhaustive list of general eye-tracking findings is beyond the scope of this book – and context and goals can also play a role in how people see a particular visual – here are some of the main findings of relevance to advertising:

- In print ads, for every 1 per cent increase in the size of the ad on the page there is a 0.8 per cent increase in gaze duration (in feature ads this connection appears to be much weaker, with only a 0.22 per cent increase in gaze duration for every 1 per cent increase in size).[3]

- If someone's attention is drawn to the brand logo of an ad, it will tend to 'spill over' onto the image and the text, but not vice versa. Similarly, attention grabbed by the image will spill over onto the text but not vice versa.[4]

- People display a general bias towards looking longer at curved objects as opposed to pointy or straight ones (both in terms of edges and corners).[5]

- The more visually complex or informative an ad, the more attention it receives.[6]

- In TV ads, displaying the brand on-screen tends to disperse attention and increase the likelihood of changing channels.[7]

- When consumers are trying to find a particular brand of product on the supermarket shelves, they will tend to use only one or two basic features such as colours to guide their search (again highlighting the importance of brands being visually distinctive in order to be discoverable). They will also tend to look more at the centre of packages than the edges (as more useful and identifying information is expected to reside there).[8]

- Web users often scan a page using an 'F-shaped' scan path, with one horizontal movement across the top of the page, then they move down a bit and again scan from left to right, but a little bit shorter distance across the screen, finally followed by a slow horizontal scan down the left side of the page.[9] However, some now believe that this pattern is not used, and was more an artefact of how web browsers used to view Google search results.

- There is some evidence that, perhaps contrary to expectations, faces and imagery sometimes get less attention than text in an ad. This may be because viewers are searching for the most information-rich areas of an ad.[10] Nevertheless, faces, particularly ones expressing an emotion, can be good for grabbing initial attention, or directing the viewers' attention on to other salient areas of the image.

- Some commercial research with web users has uncovered what might be termed the rule of one-third: users typically only look at one-third of ads online, and for each ad they typically only look at it for one-third of a second.[11]

If a design appears cluttered and the information that the consumer is interested in has to be searched out effortfully, it may be less effective than if the design is clear and distinct, with an arrangement of information that allows the consumer to grasp what they need to know quickly and easily.

Fixation predicts choice

One of the most interesting potential sources of eye-tracking insight for marketers and advertisers is the ability to predict choices. There is some evidence that fixation can predict which of a number of items a person will choose. For example, one study found that when participants were asked to pick the most attractive of a series of faces, or a series of logos, the one they picked received the longest fixation time.[12]

With print ads, we can choose to look at them or ignore them. When in the supermarket, we have to visually search a display and then may look back and forth between options to compare before we make a choice. Then, as we look more closely at a package, we will be extracting the bits of information from its imagery and text that help us to decide if we want it. All these behaviours are measurable with ET.

CASE STUDY   Using eye-tracking for media optimization

The London-based company Lumen Research (**http://www.lumen-research.com/**) runs weekly eye-tracking studies for their clients, who include magazine and newspaper companies, advertisers and advertising agencies. Over the course of more than 1,500 studies they have built a database that allows them to model the likely patterns of attention within different media.

For example, given a particular newspaper, their models allow them to predict which areas within the paper (eg side of the page, position on the page, size of ad) are most likely to receive most attention for different types of ads and different demographic groups. There are a couple of forces driving this. First, the different spatial patterns of where people are more likely to look; second, the effect of context: if an ad is next to an article that is itself generating a lot of attention, then some of this attention will 'rub off' on the ad.

One example of how Lumen has used this is a study they conducted on the press advertising bought by the seven main UK supermarket retailers around Christmas. By comparing the amounts of money spent by each supermarket on advertising space with their own metrics on size, position and actual levels of consumer engagement with the ads (from eye-tracking data), Lumen were able to quantify the different amounts of engagement per £1 spent for each brand. The most efficient advertiser was Tesco, as even though they spent considerably less than the top-spending advertiser (£2.4 million versus £3.8 million) they managed to achieve the same overall amount of 'dwell time' of readers looking at their ads. Smart use of placement and size of ads, combined with good creative design, saved them approximately £1.4 million.

David Bassett, director of analytics at Lumen, says: 'Our models have revealed there is a gap between how advertising space is currently priced, and what it is worth. In other words it is inefficiently priced. By doing this kind of work we've enabled both advertisers to optimize where they place their ads, and media owners to understand the value of their space.'

Pros and cons

ET is comparably cheap, and requires little complex knowledge to generate outputs. The fundamental challenge or limitation of ET is that it shows where someone looked, but not necessarily why. Someone's gaze may have dwelt on a particular area because they found it interesting, because they found it hard to understand, or simply because they were resting their eyes there whilst thinking what to do next or covertly shifting their attention to an adjacent area.

It does not give information on the emotional feelings that a stimulus evoked, or on the meaning that it communicated (although it can be indicative of which aspects, if any, of the image are likely to be remembered). Thus, whilst it can be useful to see where a persons' eyes fixated, this information is not always conclusive.

Checklist

Running an eye-tracking study

Do you want your participants to just look at the imagery, or actively search for something? For example, for most print ads you probably just want the participants to freely look at them in order to see where their eyes move and fixate. However, in a study showing a supermarket display you may want to decide between letting participants gaze freely (to see what captures their attention) or to actively search for a particular product or brand. Nevertheless, even when gazing freely it can be useful to get participants to imagine a context or scenario in which they would be looking at the material. How we look at things is often context dependent, for example if we are more or less time-pressured (eg flicking through a newspaper quickly on a workday, compared to browsing more slowly on a weekend).

Will all the details on your images/video be legible at the size that they will be displayed to people in the test? Is there, for example, small-print text that they might not be able to read, or would have to strain to read? This could cause them to have longer fixations on those areas just because they are taking longer to make sense of it. If you have a large image size that also contains a lot of detail that it is important for people to be able to see, you may want to consider bringing people into a central location and testing using a high-definition or large screen.

Don't show people too much in one sitting. The more you show them, the more bored they are likely to become. This effect should always be counteracted by rotating the order in which you show the images/photos – and also avoid showing the same people very similar images (which will fatigue them more quickly and probably get them to look at the images in an unnatural way as they then begin to specifically search for differences between the images).

When choosing an eye-tracking provider, consider:

☐ Do you need the extra control that a lab-based study provides or would you rather have the speed and lower cost of an online study?

☐ What outputs do they provide, and what does each output actually show?

☐ If tempted to use mobile eye-tracking, consider whether the extra time and money are really necessary. Could you test your research question with images or photos instead?

Summary

- Vision is driven by both top-down and bottom-up processes.
- Eye-tracking is a comparatively cheap and unobtrusive measure.
- Eye-tracker studies are typically either lab-based, mobile or online, each with their own benefits and limitations.

Notes

1 See page 59 of: Murch, W (2001) *In the Blink of an Eye*, Silman-James Press, Los Angeles.

2 Yoo, CY (2009) Effects beyond click-through: incidental exposure to web advertising, *Journal of Marketing Communications*, **15** (4), pp 227–46.

3 Pieters, R and Wedel, M (2004) Attention capture and transfer in advertising: brand, pictoral and text-size effects, *Journal of Marketing*, **68**, pp 36–50.

4 See: Wedel, M and Pieters, R (2008) *Eye Tracking for Visual Marketing*, Now Publishing, London.

5 Amir, O, Biederman, I and Hayworth, KJ (2011) The neural basis for shape preference, *Vision Research*, **51**, pp 2198–206.

6 See: Wedel, M and Pieters, R (2008) *Eye Tracking for Visual Marketing*, Now Publishing, London.

7 Teixeira, T, Wedel, M and Pieters, R (2008) Moment-to-Moment Optimal Branding in TV Commercials: Preventing Avoidance by Pulsing, Working Paper, University of Michigan.

8 Van der Lans, R, Pieters, R and Wedel, M (2008) Competitive brand salience, *Marketing Science*, **27** (5), pp 922–31.

9 Nielsen, J [accessed 24 April 2015] *F-Shaped Pattern for Reading Web Content* [Online] http://www.nngroup.com/articles/f-shaped-pattern-reading-web-content/.

10 Eyequant [accessed 24 April 2015] Eye-Tracking study [Online] http://blog.eyequant.com/2014/01/15/the-3-most-surprising-insights-from-a-200-website-eye-tracking-study/. Other vendors I've spoken to disagree that faces aren't effective.

11 Nielsen, Jakob and Pernice, Kara (2010) *Eyetracking Web Usability*, New Riders, Berkeley, CA.

12 Glaholt, MG, Wu, M and Reingold, EM (2009) Predicting preference from fixations, *PsychNology*, **7** (12), pp 141–58.

IMPLICIT RESPONSE MEASURES 07

Have you ever bought a new item of clothing or maybe a car and suddenly you see the same item or car wherever you go? The more recently familiar we are with things, the more easily we notice them. This familiarity extends to all the things we associate with something too. For example, if you are asked to look at a picture of a jar of coffee and are then asked to guess what the missing letter is that makes this into a word – c_p – you are more likely to guess that the word is 'cup', whereas if you had previously been exposed to images of hats, you would probably be more likely to pick 'cap'.

This would happen even if you were not trying to second-guess the intention behind asking you to do this apparently contrived task! It is happening at an automatic, system 1, non-conscious level. Also, these types of fill-in-the-missing-parts tasks are something that our non-conscious minds are doing all the time as we navigate the world around us. This is the phenomenon of priming, mentioned in Chapter 3.

Implicit memory webs

Non-conscious connections can be thought of as implicit memory webs (also sometimes known in marketing as a 'brand engram'), and they connect together things that we have come to believe share some kind of similarity. Implicit connections are activated automatically, but they are not like knee-jerk instinctive reactions, such as jumping at the sight of a snake; they are built through experience. If things are repeatedly seen or experienced at the same time, if they sound similar, or cause us to think and feel similar things, they become woven together in a net of familiarity: tug on one and the others also move. Words, concepts, logos, even colours and type fonts can become linked through such repetitive contiguity. These linkages can be strong with established brands, such that if you see a particular shade of red, green or purple, Coca-Cola, Garnier or Cadbury may come to mind. Such elements become part of a brand's identity and are useful at point of sale, or moment of purchase, as their familiarity, or association with positive feelings, can help sway (although not impel) a consumer towards that brand (this is a part of what Byron Sharp means by making a brand 'distinct', as we discussed in Chapter 2). Such connections can be built up through our own personal experiences with a brand, product or service, through the things that we hear others say about it, and through the brand's own communications.

If we consider a brand such as Apple, it is likely that most people who are aware of Apple will have some form of mental network of associations with the brand that might be similar to that shown in Figure 7.1.

Note that a brand's implicit memory web not only includes its products and the categories it operates in, but sensory things such as colours or the feel of its products, people, emotions and behaviour patterns that we associate with it. Note also that this is just a simplified illustration. It is likely that we have many more connections with any particular brand.

These networks of associations mean that brands and ads tend to automatically trigger collections of meanings and emotions that were not obviously, explicitly there. Implicit brand memory webs are a system

FIGURE 7.1 Simplified example of a web of implicit brand associations; the closer the concept is to the central brand, the stronger its connection to it

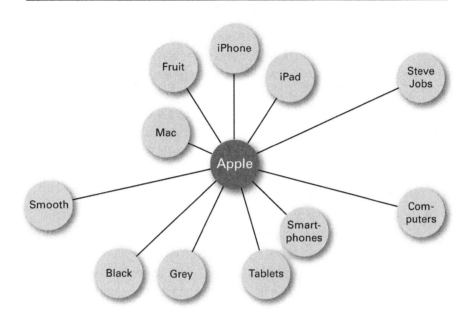

1 time-and-energy-saving shortcut: if we can just instantly 'feel' our stored attitude towards something like a product, built up of past experience, then we can avoid having to do the work of re-evaluating or thinking through our attitudes each time we have to make a choice. Having a favourable implicit attitude towards a product is not only likely to draw us towards it but to make the choice itself feel more effortless.

There is some evidence to suggest that implicit (system 1) processes are most likely to influence choices when consumers are in a rush or making fast decisions. For example, in one study, when participants had to make a choice between different writing pads, their implicit attitudes were predictive only when they had to choose within five seconds.[1]

It is not exactly known how implicit memory works in the brain, and there are different theories being debated to explain it. Also, it is likely that there are different types of implicit memory that different tests tap. For example, there may be different implicit memory systems for perceptual (the way things look, sound or feel) and conceptual (the underlying meaning of things) information. Seeing or holding one of a brand's products may trigger a slightly different set of associations from merely thinking about the brand.

However, there are a number of features of implicit memory that we know about that are relevant to marketers:

- *It increases the feeling of ease and familiarity*: in one study people were asked to read a series of unfamiliar brand names. A day later, when shown some of the names again, they were more likely to believe that they were well-known brands, even if they could not consciously remember having seen them the day before. It was their mere implicit memory familiarity that caused the feeling that they must be well-known.[2] Bearing in mind what we know about people liking things that they find familiar (see Chapter 3), this is particularly important for brands.

- *It works in the background*: in one study on product placement in TV shows, results showed different patterns for explicit and implicit memory. Whilst having the placement shown prominently was more effective for explicit memory, it wasn't the case for the implicit measure. When it comes to implicit effectiveness, subtlety works as well as or better than obviousness.[3]

- *It is separate from our conscious memory system*: our implicit memory system is separate from our conscious memory (eg we can recognize more things that we can consciously, wilfully recall). Hence it is not directly measurable through questioning – we have to infer it through other measures.

  One example of this is with those who have apparently lost their memory: amnesiacs. Studies have shown that memory-impaired amnesiacs who struggle to learn new lists of words when explicitly questioned nevertheless show increased implicit learning for those words – showing that not only is implicit memory effectively a separate memory system, but one for which we do not have full conscious awareness.[4]

Academic underpinning

The very earliest studies of implicit memory may have been by the German psychologist Hermann Ebbinghaus in the 19th century. He asked people to learn some material, and then got them to forget it (eg by leaving some time) then later asked them to learn it a second time. Their existing implicit familiarity with the material made it easier – and hence faster – to learn the second time.

This time-based measurement provides one way to show how subsequent measures of implicit memory work. Congruent concepts make thinking faster, like skating on ice; incongruent concepts make thinking slower, like wading through mud. So if we give someone a task, we should be able to make them slower or faster according to whether we present them with congruent or dissonant pairings of words or images.

In the 1990s psychologists became interested in studying implicit attitudes, and began to develop tests that used reaction times to probe how closely connected different concepts were in participants' minds (there are also other types of implicit tests). Such tests (known as sequential priming measures) have been shown to correlate significantly with behaviour.[5]

As implicit attitudes are thought to be less subject to self-censorship in the face of social unacceptability, the focus of academic research has largely been on areas of implicit social biases, such as racial stereotyping, which may not reveal themselves so easily through conscious questioning.

Probably the most widely studied and academically evaluated implicit techniques have been the Implicit Association Test (IAT) and affective priming.[6]

The Implicit Association Test (IAT)

The IAT was developed in the 1990s by the psychologist Anthony Greenwald and colleagues, who later developed a web-based, non-profit organization for encouraging research and education on implicit social cognition, called Project Implicit. You can visit the Project Implicit web page and try an IAT test for yourself at: **https://implicit.harvard.edu/implicit**.

I'll describe it here purely as a general example of an implicit test. In reality, the exact test designs used by marketers will often be different, as the IAT has rights restrictions for non-commercial use.

The test involves a double-categorization task where participants are given four categories, two that are usually 'unpleasant' or 'pleasant' (or the equivalent) and another two that are concept- or object-related (ie related to the subject being studied – for example, cats and dogs). Words or images representing each category (eg pleasant, unpleasant, cats, dogs) will be displayed on the centre of a computer screen and the participant will have to classify the word according to which category it fits, by pressing a computer key (eg E or I) whose position corresponds to whether the category is to be sorted to the left or right of the screen (see Figure 7.2).

Blocks 1 and 2: the test typically begins with a couple of practice trials, one for the pleasant/unpleasant categorization, the other for the subject categorization – eg cats or dogs. The words that flash up in the centre of the screen will in one case be either words that can be categorized as pleasant or unpleasant, or words that relate to cats or to dogs.
   Once the person has got used to the task through the practice trials, they then move on to the third block (in which data is now being collected).

Blocks 3 and 4: in the third block the two categories are now combined in some way. So, for example, the person may see words from either category; if they see a pleasant or dog word, they press E, if they see an unpleasant or cat word they press I. There is then a fourth block, which repeats the first block but is longer.

Block 5: in the fifth block the task is the same but the combination of categories is now mixed up. So, for example, it may be that if 'dog' was on the left in block one (or the E key) it would now appear on the right (or I key) and the opposite for 'cat'.

Blocks 6 and 7: the sixth block then repeats the third, but with the categories reversed. Then the seventh repeats the sixth, but with more trials.

As you have probably guessed, it is the degree of implicit congruity or disparity between the two categories (eg dogs and cats) and the positive or negative labels that affects people's speed of response.

Benefits of the IAT include: easy to use, gives large effect sizes and has good reliability.[7] One of the criticisms of the IAT is that it is inherently comparative, measuring two concepts together but unable to give measurements of each in isolation.[8]

Furthermore, the IAT has been criticized for introducing block order bias. Some variants on the IAT that attempt to address these problems have been developed but they have not yet been as rigorously validated as the IAT.

FIGURE 7.2 A typical IAT procedure

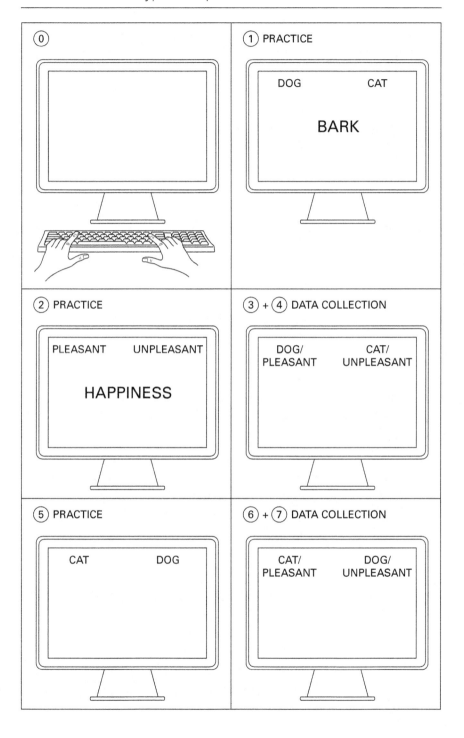

Affective and evaluative priming tests

There are other implicit-reaction research paradigms such as affective or evaluative priming tests (the two terms refer to the same basic testing paradigm).[9] In these tests the participants are sorting target words or images (such as brand names or product examples) into one of two categories (rather than the four of the IAT) such as brand A or B.

An example of an affective priming test would be where images (such as logos or bottles) or words (such as brand names) representing wine brand A or B flash up on the screen and the participant has to categorize them according to which brand they are. However, before each brand word or image appears it is briefly preceded by a word that might be an adjective such as 'premium', 'trendy', 'passionate' or 'irritating'. The variations in how long it takes people to categorize the brand are influenced by the degree of connection between the brand and the prime word that preceded it. For example, a lover of brand A might be faster to categorize a logo as belonging to this brand when it is preceded by the word 'delicious' rather than the word 'disgusting'.

In another variant of this test the participant is sorting between words that are unambiguously good or bad (or two extremes of a positive versus negative construct such as 'high quality versus low quality'),[10] and is being primed by words that they will likely have a positive or negative affinity for, such as brand names that they likely associate as being good/bad or high quality/low quality – ie there are some test designs where the brands or products are the primes, and some where they are the targets.

One advantage of affective priming tests is that they are easier to design so that you can evaluate brands separately (rather than in a purely joint comparison test).[11] One of the differences between the IAT and affective priming techniques is that IATs seem to be better suited to measuring categories, whilst affective priming is better at measuring particular examples of categories.

Some market research priming tests include exposure to a stimulus, which could be a still image or a short video (such as a TV ad) sandwiched in-between two identical tests. This is called an intervention stimulus, and is used to see if it shifts the automatic associations measured in the pre-test to the post-test. For example, participants might complete an affective priming test to measure their associations with two wine brands, then they view a TV ad for one of the brands, then complete the same priming test again. The average reaction times for the same prime-target pairs can be compared across the first (pre) and second (post) tests to see what differences there are. Any significant differences are then taken to have been caused by the ad that the participants watched in-between.

Their use for marketers

Market researchers are increasingly using these types of tests, either one of the standard academically tested paradigms, or a more bespoke one. You can either commission a specialist agency to run a test, or code one yourself. If the latter, there are platforms such as MediaLab, Micro-Experimental Laboratory (MEL), PsyScope, or Inquisit in which tests can be created, or they can be directly coded in languages such as Java, PHP, Flash etc.

These measures can be useful to marketers in mapping out which areas they should push into, and which to stay clear of, which words to use, and which to avoid. Similar to the concept of 'paving the cowpath' in Chapter 4, they can show us which combinations of ideas feel most natural to consumers.

Implicit measures may be particularly useful for studying 'vice' consumer behaviours: eg those relating to tempting (but unhealthy) foods, smoking or alcohol. In these areas there is often strong pressure to either deceive oneself, or to appear virtuous when questioned, either for reasons of vanity or social desirability.

One study, for example, examined attitudes in Poland towards Polish versus foreign brands across a number of product categories. Whilst explicit questioning showed that the Polish consumers preferred the US brands, the implicit questioning showed a more favourable rating for the Polish ones.[12]

This example of what psychologists call 'in-group bias' (favouring a group of which you are a member) maybe affects consumers' implicit attitudes not just to the country of origin of a brand, but of spokespeople, or of whether they are associating a brand with themselves or not. Consumers may be unaware of these biases, or just embarrassed to admit to them when questioned!

Brand-mapping

Implicit tests are ideal for brand-mapping and positioning research. Brand planners tend to work with words; their brand is defined by a collection of words, so implicit techniques quantify the exact thing that they already work with. Regular implicit testing can be a good way to track the brand's evolution over time, and to make sure that it is still projecting the right things to consumers. Another use of brand-mapping is to understand the territories of meaning that your brand occupies relative to its competitors. This can reveal areas of uniqueness or differentiation, as well as how well you are evoking qualities that your competitor is also evoking (you can test your competitor's brand as well). Another area of brand-mapping that implicit testing can be used for is to gauge the degree of association between your brand and potential new areas of brand extension. For example, if your brand is a supermarket, how closely is it connected to other service categories such as banking or insurance? A close connection could point to an easier potential for a brand to move into that business than a weaker connection. If an established brand can extend into new products then those products have the advantage of the instant recognition and familiarity that come with the brand, and are effective in system 1 success.

Testing whether an ad fulfils its aims

Another of the most frequent uses of implicit testing is in ad testing. Other techniques often focus on the moment-by-moment effect of an ad on emotions, memory and attention, whereas the focus of implicit response measures is on measuring whether and to what degree an ad evokes the specific concepts and emotions that it was intended to. One downside to this type of testing is that it tends to give overall scores for the ad, without the moment-by-moment diagnostics. If a particular concept fails or succeeds to be communicated by the ad, the test will not tell you which sections need to be changed, or which were responsible. Nevertheless, it is often relatively easy to infer this. The real power of using implicit measures for ad testing may be for testing several competing versions of an ad against each other to see which best communicates the desired attributes.

Media-mapping

A more complex, yet in-demand, question that implicit testing can address is the potential for different media to communicate different emotions and concepts. In other words, if you take the same campaign, and the same range of attribute words, which medium (eg TV, radio, print) is better at evoking each attribute? Whilst this is possible, in practice it means a comparatively large (and hence more costly) test. If your question is just relating to one campaign (eg given campaign A, how does it perform across each medium?) then the test may be relatively normal in size. However, if you are trying to answer the larger question of how different media perform in general, across multiple campaigns, then you will need to test a lot more material as well as use more sophisticated testing designs.

Price-testing

Implicit tests can be used to measure the degree of association between a product and a price. Rather than attribute words, price figures are shown. This is effectively showing which price(s) feels most natural in consumers' minds.

Some watch-outs

When building or commissioning implicit tests, here are a few things to consider:

- A true implicit test does not allow for deliberation, however quick. Instead, participants are focused on completing a task, as opposed to proffering a quick opinion. It is almost impossible for people to consciously, systematically control their implicit responses. They cannot wilfully second-guess, self-censor or edit their responses in the way they can with typical articulated research. Simply asking people to categorize something quickly may be better than articulated research, but it is not a true implicit test.

- Nevertheless, it is likely that there is no sharp demarcation between how implicit and explicit memories and attitudes affect us in the real world. It is likely that they form a continuum.

- Bear in mind that whilst these measures offer apparent precision that does not necessarily mean they can precisely distinguish very closely matched words. Whilst marketing teams might agonize and debate over the finest shades of difference between words to describe their brand, it does not mean that such tight demarcations of meaning exist in the consumers' minds, and there may sometimes be a high degree of variation between consumers on this.

- Also, just because you theorize that a particular word is important to driving sales, and you then find that your brand strongly implicitly activates that word, it does not follow that you will definitely have strong sales. You need to first establish what words/concepts are genuinely driving your consumers.

- Negativity-bias is the tendency for negative words to be recognized faster than positive ones. Usually it's best not to mix in one negative word when all the others are positive.

Implicit testing terms

Prime: this is the word or image that you are using to activate the participants' response to the target.

Target: the words or images that the participant is being asked to categorize or respond to.

The intervention stimulus: some formats of implicit testing prime participants with exposure to an image, video or sound clip sandwiched in-between two tests in order to see the pre- versus post-difference (from which you can then infer the effect of the stimulus on the priming scores).

Trial: one instance of the test in which participants must press a key to make a choice.

Block: a series of trials.

Effect size: the statistical measure of the strength of connection between the attribute and the brand.

Statistical power size: how likely the results are to be due to a genuine connection between the prime and the target.

Checklist

Decoding an implicit study

☐ *Choosing stimuli*: when using category examples you have to first test them to make sure they are representative of the category. People may respond differently to different examples, and hence they might not be acting as a pure 'proxy' measure for the category itself.

One interesting way to choose your attribute words, if time and money allow, might be to first conduct some research on the types of words that your target market are already using in relation to your brand or ad campaigns.

Try (as far as possible) to control for word frequency and length. In reality this is not absolutely achievable, particularly with length, but it is a good constraint to aim at, even if it's not fully achieved.

☐ *Semantic syllables*: in the same way that words can have syllables (and hence take longer to say, the more syllables they have) words can have multiple layers of meaning that take longer to process. For this reason, a word like 'non-smoker' would take longer to process than 'smoker' as it involves putting together two concepts. Ideally use only words that involve one concept to understand.

☐ *Consider using groups of attributes*: the danger with using one particular word to measure a concept is that it may be that your participants are not all interpreting the word in the same way you are. Having multiple attribute words that are all pointing towards a larger concept can minimize the chance that your results are just quirks of how people are interpreting just one word.

☐ *Consider using factor analysis*: whilst you can make a best guess at creating groups of attributes, it may be that in your consumers' minds they are grouped quite differently. Factor analysis of the data can reveal how the attributes are clustering together in the consumers' implicit memory webs. This exercise alone can yield insights into your consumers, as it can show not only which concepts are being more or less closely associated with your brand, but...

☐ *How to present the results*: as implicit studies give numerical results, and typically all on one scale, the data is often available in such a format that the end user can graph it however they like, in a typical spreadsheet program such as Microsoft Excel. Bar, column and radar graphs are usually the best formats to use.

CASE STUDY   Comparing advertising across media

Global Radio, the biggest commercial radio group in the UK, felt that radio's potential as an advertising medium had not been fully recognized. For example, some advertisers tend to assume that radio can only deliver tactical advertising messages (eg short-term, information-based ads, such as '10% off this weekend at our store').

They wanted to commission some exploratory research that would help reveal the full spectrum of radio's strengths, particularly in communicating brands' emotional aspects.

Therefore, a methodology was needed that could measure a wide array of qualities of the ads, so implicit response was chosen. Next, several campaigns needed to be selected that ran across each of the different media. One campaign alone would not be enough as any results could be more due to quirks of its content than differences between the media themselves. Campaigns were selected from a supermarket, a bank and a shampoo brand. Each had radio, TV and print.

Over 1,500 respondents (both male and female, and across a range of ages) were recruited online and first had to complete a short profiling questionnaire to qualify. They were then directed to a page where an implicit response test had been constructed by the specialist agency Neurosense. The test exposed each participant to one of the nine ads, and then they completed an implicit response task, in which they had to sort icons into two categories, one icon of which was representative of the ad. Just before each icon appeared, one of around 50 attribute words flashed up. The attributes had been carefully selected to communicate one of several different qualities that advertising typically seeks to evoke (eg intent to purchase, enjoyment, dependability and good product functionality).

Neurosense then filtered the data, and statistically transformed it into an association index (with higher values representing closer association between each word and the ad). A factor analysis was also performed on the data that showed how the individual words naturally grouped together into categories (as opposed to the original categories that had been defined). This revealed a number of areas in which the radio ads were strong, compared to the versions of the ads in other media.

Kate Rutter, head of commercial insights at Global Radio, believes that the implicit testing methodology gave them some key insights into the relative power of radio as an advertising medium:

The findings of the research enabled us to uncover the implicit strengths of each medium. We were able to see that radio advertising has important strengths with consumers in terms of trust, and intent to purchase.

Using implicit research has given us the evidence we need to support what we have always known – not only can radio drive tactical advertising but it is also an important asset for branding campaigns, delivering personal and emotional resonance. As a result of these findings we are looking to complement our traditional explicit campaign effectiveness offering with implicit methodologies.

Pros and cons

To conclude, here are some of the benefits and drawbacks of implicit testing for marketers.

Pros

The technique is comparatively fast and cheap. It can be conducted online with people at home who have computers with keyboards. Vendors are also increasingly offering implicit testing on tablet/smartphone platforms.

It measures the thing that marketers are often most interested in: brand or ad attributes as expressed in words.

As it is using words, its outputs are flexible and rich. Researchers are not pushed into trying to answer their particular question with a pre-existing batch of metrics that relate to psychological constructs (such as a vendor's measures of attention or engagement).

It is possible to graph the results in a unit that is very close to milliseconds. Therefore, the results are more intuitive to understand for marketers as they do not use abstract indexes that are far removed from what was observably measured.

Cons

Whilst the technique puts all participants onto a common measurement scale (something that a typical survey would find harder, as it would suffer from the 'noise' of how people scale their own responses) it still may be hard to compare results across cultures as the words used may differ in meaning.

Whilst implicit tests are good at giving overall readings for audiovisual experiences such as ads, they are typically not able to give second-by-second measures of them. Therefore, they lack the more precise diagnostic results for knowing how to optimize an ad by recutting it.

In order to measure experiences that cannot be captured on-screen (such as reactions to the physical features of packaging, or products that require consumers to touch them) you will need to run an 'in lab' study, therefore losing the benefits of cheapness and speed that an online study can provide (although this is true of any technique).

Some have argued that implicit influences on our buying behaviour must be small. For example, everyone is exposed to the same bewildering array of messages in the supermarket – all pulling in different directions, they would likely cancel one another out! However, whilst the effects of implicit advertising may be small (one review of 23 studies found a tiny overall effect size, yet still one that was larger than the effect of aspirin on heart attacks),[13] its effects are more to 'oil the gears' of our mental machinery, to make some choices just that bit easier and smoother than others. In other words to gently edge the odds in favour of one brand over another, even though these implicit effects do not have the power of outright persuasion. Also, in advertising, the effects are likely cumulative over time. Implicit effects work to enhance rather than enforce.

Summary

- Implicit response tests do not directly ask participants for their opinions, but instead pair concepts together and see how the different pairings either slow down or speed up simple categorization tasks.

- The participants' reaction speeds on each pairing become a measurement of the degree of association between the two concepts.

- There are a number of different implicit testing paradigms. The academic ones mostly test binary or positive versus negative-type associations, whereas many of the market research paradigms test the connection between a wide array of attributes and a brand or ad.

- Implicit response tests are a powerful and versatile way of measuring the degree to which important qualities are being automatically evoked by a brand, ad, service or product.

Notes

1 Plessner, H, Wanke, M, Harr, T and Friese, M (2004) Implicit Consumer Attitudes and their Influence on Brand Choice. Unpublished manuscript. Also see Wanke, M, Plessner, H and Friese, M (2002) When Implicit Attitudes Predict Brand-Choice and When They Don't. Paper presented at the Asia-Pacific Advances in Consumer Research conference.

2 Holden, SJS and Vanheule, M (1999) Know the name, forget the exposure: brand familiarity versus memory of exposure context, *Psychology & Marketing*, **16** (6), pp 479–96.

3 Law, S and Braun, KA (2000) I'll have what she's having: gauging the impact of product placements on viewers, *Psychology and Marketing*, **17**, pp 1059–75.

4 For example, see: Goshen-Gottstein, Y, Morris, M and Brenda, M (2000) Intact implicit memory for newly formed verbal associations in amnesic patients following single study trials, *Neuropsychology*, **14** (4), pp 570–78.

5 Cameron, CD, Brown-Iannuzzi, JL and Payne, BK (2012) Sequential priming measures of implicit social cognition: a meta-analysis of associations with behaviour and explicit attitudes, *Personality and Social Psychology Review*, **16** (4), pp 330–50.

6 Rudman, LA (2011) Implicit measures for social and personality psychology, Sage, London.

7 Greenwald, AG and Nosek, BA (2001) Health of the implicit association test at age 3, *Zeitschrift für Experimentelle Psychologie*, **48**, pp 85–93.

8 Nosek, BA, Greenwald, AG and Banaji, MR (2005) Understanding and using the Implicit Association Test: II: method variables and construct validity, *Personality and Social Psychology Bulletin*, **31** (2), pp 166–80.

9 Personal communication with Russell Fazio.

10 Reid, A [accessed 24 April 2015] Protecting the Science, *Sentient Decision Science* [Online] http://www.sentientdecisionscience.com/evaluative-priming-consumer-insights-protecting-science/.

11 Wittenbrink, B (2007) Measuring attitudes through priming, in *Implicit Measures of Attitudes*, ed B Wittenbrink and N Schwarz, Guilford Press, New York.

12 See Perkins, A, Forehand, M, Greenwald, A and Maison, D (2008) Measuring the nonconscious implicit social cognition in consumer behavior, *Handbook of Consumer Psychology*, ed CP Haugtvedt, P Herr and F Kardes, Chapter 17, Psychology Press, New York.

13 Trappey, C (1996) A meta-analysis of consumer choice and subliminal advertising, *Psychology and Marketing*, **13** (5), pp 517–30.

FACIAL ACTION CODING

Emotions are often vitally important to effective marketing, yet can be difficult to measure. Academic debates still persist about how to classify emotions and feelings, and how to disentangle their biological, neurological and social causes. For example, where do emotions begin: in the body or the brain? And if it is a mixture, under which conditions does each dominate? Or, to what extent do we learn our emotions, and to what extent are they biologically inherited? Questions like these have made emotions tricky to grasp, yet there is one area of emotional measurement that is reasonably clear: facial expressions.

We probably evolved facial expressions as a way to signal to others our feelings and intentions. They also act to intensify or enhance our own feelings (eg experiments have shown that even activating the muscles that enable us to smile can make us feel happy). Humans are both very interested in faces, and good at decoding the meanings of different facial expressions. It has been estimated that we can make more than 10,000 facial expressions,[1] although most will be combinations of and variations on a smaller number of key expressions.

As far back as the 19th century Charles Darwin, in his book *The Expression of Emotions in Man and Animals* (1872), had argued that emotions were innate and universal. However, in the 20th century the prevailing view amongst psychologists became that emotional expressions were learned and hence merely a product of the culture in which we grew up.

In the 1970s the psychologist Paul Ekman and his colleagues catalogued the activations of different facial muscles and how they produced emotional expressions. They published a manual for researchers to learn to observe the facial movements of a person (either live or via video) and code them according to this emotional taxonomy. Their Facial Action Coding System (often referred to as FACS) is based around understanding the different actions of 43 facial muscles. This is a key point: the basic units of their system are not the muscles themselves, nor the expressions themselves, but the frequently occurring combinations of muscle movements that create a facial action. These facial actions include such motions as wrinkling of the nose, raising of the cheeks and raising of the inner or outer brow. They have names such as 'inner brow raiser' and 'lip corner depressor'. Varying combinations of these muscles' actions produce unique facial emotions. Focusing on the underlying muscle movements helps to avoid the challenges posed by variations between people in the shape and detail of their faces. The details of a person's face may vary, but to smile we all use the same muscles. The muscle actions, like the notes of a musical scale, or the genes in a DNA strand, comprise a language.

The six primary emotions

It was also then found that a selection of six 'primary' emotional expressions seem to be universal across different cultures. These are anger, disgust, fear, happiness, sadness and surprise (sometimes 'contempt' is also included) (see Figure 8.1).[2] The previous dominant theory that facial emotions were social constructs that we learn from our culture meant that they may vary from country to country. Whilst this may be true for some emotions, it does seem that the core six listed here are pan-cultural, and hence most likely inherited more than learned. Whether you were brought up in a developed nation with access to mass media, or are a remote tribesperson without televisual contact, you will likely be able to correctly recognize each of those six faces.[3] Indeed, in support of the idea that these expressions are biologically inherited is the fact that FACS has also been used, with adaptation, with chimpanzees!

Whilst these basic six expressions can be thought of as primary, they can also appear in combination to create secondary facial expressions. For example, if you hear an amusing yet repulsive joke, your face can show a combination of happiness and disgust simultaneously. Such combinations are sometimes called compound emotions. They have not yet had such

FIGURE 8.1 The six universal emotions in the FACS

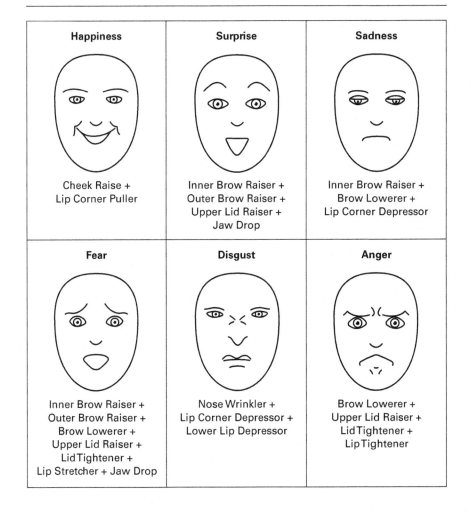

Happiness	Surprise	Sadness
Cheek Raise + Lip Corner Puller	Inner Brow Raiser + Outer Brow Raiser + Upper Lid Raiser + Jaw Drop	Inner Brow Raiser + Brow Lowerer + Lip Corner Depressor
Fear	**Disgust**	**Anger**
Inner Brow Raiser + Outer Brow Raiser + Brow Lowerer + Upper Lid Raiser + Lid Tightener + Lip Stretcher + Jaw Drop	Nose Wrinkler + Lip Corner Depressor + Lower Lip Depressor	Brow Lowerer + Upper Lid Raiser + Lid Tightener + Lip Tightener

extensive cross-cultural testing as the main six emotions, and even within the culture that they were tested (North America) they seem to be slightly less universally recognized than the main six. So there is likely a spectrum of facial emotions, from the most universal (the basic six) to those which are fairly universal (such as the compound emotions) to the more culturally specific or idiosyncratic.

Interestingly, Paul Ekman has argued that these six emotions begin involuntarily, suggesting that they are triggered non-consciously and are even more powerful than our basic drives (eg food, procreation) because they can trump them. For example, disgust can override hunger; sudden onset of fear can override procreation. Of course, these core emotions are probably at the extreme end of the inherited versus idiosyncratic spectrum. Also, broadly speaking, whilst in everyday language we may use these words interchangeably, psychologists tend to distinguish between the following:

- *Emotions*: the bodily component of our emotional experience. Often these can be fleeting, lasting only seconds or less.

- *Feelings*: the inner experiences we have (which may be the same as emotions, ie be caused by them, or may cause emotions).

- *Moods*: general emotional 'background' that may last hours or longer.

As the six core facial emotions are so fundamental, the assumption is that they are also universally mirrored by the expected inner feelings of each emotion. Interestingly, FACS can be used in detecting deception (a difference between what we are feeling inside, and what is showing on our face). Freud wrote: 'He that has eyes to see and ears to hear may convince himself that no mortal can keep a secret. If his lips are silent, he chatters with his fingertips; betrayal oozes out of him at every pore.'[4] He may as well have added facial expressions to his list, as people's inner emotions often leak out through their face even when they don't want them to. For example, there is a muscular difference between a faked smile and a real one. Also, when we try to supress a facial expression it often leaks through quickly, for about a quarter of a second, before we are able to get it under control. These are called microexpressions, and their study is often useful in criminal cases. These are facial coding applications that go beyond typical marketing questions, but they do highlight the semi-involuntary nature of the core facial emotions, and hence their use as an often more honest communication channel than speech alone. Also, the tendency to inhibit our facial expressions may vary across cultures. For example, there is some evidence that Japanese people are more likely to inhibit smiling in social or public settings than Westerners.

Automated FACS (aFACS)

Whilst FACS has been around for years, it has been a very time-consuming process to code videos manually. Similar measurements can be made directly with sensors on the person's face, measuring the electrical activity generated when muscles become active (a technique called facial electro-myography). Whilst this can be very precise, it is obviously a more invasive process for participants, and can be costly as you have to recruit people to travel to a physical lab location.

However, in recent years systems have been developed to allow for automated facial coding via a camera and software. You may already have a camera or photo software that can automatically find faces in your photos, and sometimes even recognize who they are (interestingly, some-times these software packages suffer from the human quirk of pareidolia: the tendency to see faces in random patterns). Automated facial coding goes one step further and recognizes emotional expressions in faces as they evolve second by second. The growth of cloud-computing power, as well as the proliferation of home computers with webcams and high-speed internet, has now made it feasible to offer automated facial coding on a wide basis.

For online recruitment databases, for example, after having passed the screening questions the applicants are directed to a web link that will ac-tivate their webcam, locate their face and begin to record its movements whilst various stimuli are displayed. These could be videos or images.

There are a number of virtues of aFAC for market research. Here are some of the main ones:

- Unobtrusive: the systems do not need sensors attached to the person or require them to do anything (eg they usually do not require any calibration procedures), so participants can just view the test material naturally with nothing taxing or strange about the process.

- Fast: the process of running a study and being able to access the results is often between 24 and 48 hours.

- Intuitive, DIY dashboard: the results are usually viewable on an online dashboard in intuitive visualizations. The usual format is to have a video feedback in synch with a line graph showing the strength of each of the emotions as they ebb and flow second by second. This enables market researchers to quickly analyse results, and to see very clearly what they mean.

- Scalable: as the testing process and analysis are almost completely automated it means that the method is very scalable. There is never the problem of testing facility or analysis resources becoming scarce during busy periods.

- Additional metrics: in addition to the six core FACS emotions, some automated systems have added in extra metrics. For example, overall emotional engagement (some kind of composite score based on the existence of the six emotions at any given moment) or approach/withdrawal (the degree to which the person is emotionally attracted or repulsed by what they are seeing, depending on how much their bodies are moving towards or away from the screen. At the time of writing at least one of the main suppliers is also experimenting with reading changes in heart rate via subtle changes in the colour of the facial skin!

- Comparatively inexpensive: compared to methods such as biometrics or direct brain recordings, aFAC is inexpensive, particularly, for example, for video analysis.

Unfortunately, aFAC also has some limitations:

- Limited emotional range: currently the core six emotions are of limited use to marketers. For example, only two of them are positive emotions. Also, they are all fairly 'intense' emotions. Disgust and fear, for example, are rarely evoked by mainstream marketing communications. Nevertheless, they may have their place in more emotive materials, such as movie trailers.

- Emotional suppression: as yet there is not a comprehensive understanding of when people will suppress their facial expressions, and such as how this might vary across cultures. Even in large samples there are far smaller numbers who actually become facially expressive. For example, at any one point in a recording, it is not unusual to have less than 20 per cent of the sample expressing, and often it is more like 5 per cent or less.

However, both of these limitations are likely to be minimized over time as computing power accelerates, databases grow and understanding deepens. Also, some users are already augmenting the sensitivity of the measures through selectively adding some manual coding to the analysis (although this obviously slows down the process and increases costs).

CASE STUDY Happiness whilst web browsing

The technology company Radware developed a new way for images to load on to web pages. As web users, we are often impatient and fickle: wanting pages to load as fast as possible, or we might click away to another page. Websites are becoming increasingly image-rich, and also – particularly e-commerce sites – recognizing the importance of emotionally engaging users. When it comes to optimal image loading, there have historically been two routes: either first load a low-resolution version of the image as fast as possible, then sharpen it up, or load the full-resolution image, but more slowly. Radware's innovation was an image loading method that loads the full-resolution image but more quickly. The question is: do users notice and does it help engage them emotionally?

As part of a wider project (which also used implicit response measures) we decided to use aFACS to measure how emotional engagement moved over time in response to the web pages loading using the different image-loading techniques. We were interested in measuring happiness or amusement to cute and funny images (one of the more frequently evoked emotions via website photos) and as we needed a second-by-second metric for this reaction, the aFACS happiness trace was perfectly suited.

We chose three websites that might have these types of images: YouTube (a page listing funny cat videos, with preview images), a clothing site with images of very cute toddlers, and a greetings card website with cards depicting funny animals. We predicted that all of these pages should be smile-inducing, and also we needed a variety of site types in order to minimize the chances that any effects we found were content-specific: it was the effect of the image-loading that we were interested in, not the type of content itself. With this in mind we created videos to simulate pages loading on each of the three sites, with each of the three image-loading methods: nine videos in total. We then split our testing sample into three groups: each saw the three different websites (to maximize the variety of content they saw, and keep them from getting bored) but each using the same image-loading method (so that they were not comparing different methods on different sites).

The results gave us second-by-second measures of exactly when users started smiling, how long this was sustained for, and even its intensity. As we had these measures for exactly the same websites but using different image-loading methods, we were able to see that Radware's 'Progressive Image' technique made both men and women smile sooner in the page-loading experience, and for longer periods. The information is helping them convince the industry to adopt their method.

What it is most useful for

The heartland of the use of aFACS is emotive videos. The ability for the technique to give a moment-by-moment trace of strong emotional responses is perfect for testing emotive TV ads or movie trailers, and typically at a lower cost and faster turnaround than other metrics that give moment-by-moment traces. It may also be useful for emotive experiences that evolve over time – for example, the journey through an emotive website. Currently the online versions of aFACS are geared towards screen-based stimuli, so experiences requiring physical interaction would be more specialized and require a bespoke design (probably at additional cost). It may not be quite so appropriate for materials that might not evoke such strong emotional responses, for example package designs. However, some of the vendors would argue that they have enough understanding and sensitivity to still get a read on these.

Perhaps unsurprisingly, the main use of aFACS so far has been in studying TV ads. The method is great for giving fast feedback on the moment-to-moment performance of an ad to guide fine-tuning editing. As there is often little time between the completion of an ad and its air date, the speediness of the process is a great boon.

The method probably has great potential for future improvement. There is probably a great degree of additional emotional information in people's facial behaviour, awaiting discovery with greater computing power and higher-definition cameras. What this means is that it is likely that in the near future there will be a wider array of emotions that are measurable with aFAC. The technology will probably also have increasing applications outside market research. For example, the ability to 'take the emotional temperature' of people in a crowd – in an airport or on a street in which a riot may occur, for example – has obvious security uses.

Summary

- Building upon earlier work theorizing that there are universal facial emotions, Paul Ekman and colleagues in the 1970s developed a system for rating the existence of six universal emotions. These are happiness, surprise, disgust, fear, sadness and anger.

- Recent advances in computing power and the widespread existence of home computers with webcams mean that it is now practical to make large-scale automated facial coding recordings while people experience audiovisual material.

- Automated facial coding works by presenting materials (eg images or videos) on computer screen and tracking people's facial expressions to them via webcam. It is particularly good for emotive videos.

- The technique is comparatively cheap and fast, and, although currently limited in the numbers of emotions that it can measure, its sensitivity and reach are likely to improve in the future.

Notes

1 Ekman, P (2004) *Emotions Revealed: Understanding Faces and Feelings*, Phoenix, London

2 Some people ask why 'love' is not considered one of these universal emotions. However, it does not involve one universally recognizable facial expression, but can intensify or increase the likelihood of other facial emotions. As Paul Ekman explained in an interview with the *New York Times*: 'Romantic and parental love are more enduring than emotions, though they are highly emotionally laden. I don't just feel happy with my daughter. Sometimes I'm worried, sometimes I'm surprised, and sometimes I might feel anger. It's an attachment, not a fleeting emotional state. A mood, by the way, is different still. It doesn't last as long as an attachment, though it can last for hours or

even longer.' Available [Online] http://www.nytimes.com/2003/08/05/health/conversation-with-paul-ekman-43-facial-muscles-that-reveal-even-most-fleeting.html [accessed 24 April 2015].

3 Critics, however, have pointed out several limitations to the evidence for universality. For example, people in the studies have been given a list of emotions to pick from (rather than having to suggest emotions spontaneously), and they are given a range of posed emotional expressions to judge. Evidence seems to suggest that when people have to judge only one expression, or a spontaneous expression, their recognition rates are lower. See: Russell, JA (1994) Is there universal recognition of emotion from facial expression? A review of cross-cultural studies, *Psychological Bulletin*, **115** (1), pp 102–41; also Naab, PJ and Russell, JA (2007) Judgments of emotion from spontaneous facial expressions of New Guineans, *Emotion*, **7** (4), pp 736–44.

4 Quoted in: O'Neill, J (2010) *The Domestic Economy of the Soul: Freud's Five Case Studies*, Sage, London, p 67.

BIOMETRICS 09

Whether it be salivating over delicious-looking food in the supermarket, feeling our heart 'skip a beat' as we first spot some luxury item that we instantly want, or our palms sweating with thrilling fear as we watch a horror-movie trailer, we often feel our emotional responses in our bodies. However, these are just the reactions that we are consciously aware of. Our bodies are always reacting in subtle ways, involuntarily and below our level of conscious awareness as our levels of interest, attention and emotional engagement to the things around us rise and fall.

Whilst the brain gets a lot of attention in research, it is also part of the wider nervous system that extends throughout our bodies. The bodily part of the nervous system can also provide useful measurements. The non-conscious responses of the body often react faster than the conscious mind, its mechanisms having been wired-up earlier in our evolutionary past. For example, you may have had the experience of walking into a room in the dark and before you turn the lights on you involuntarily jump, or feel your heart rate increase as you think you see the silhouette of an intruder. As your conscious, rational mind kicks in and realizes it is just a coat hanging on a hook, or some other innocuous object, you are briefly aware of the dual nature of our emotional systems. Similarly, when we watch something scary or thrilling, such as ski-jumping on TV, our bodies can involuntarily respond, as though it were us in the risky situation. Our bodies often respond to what we are seeing on screens as though it were real, a good indicator that not only do our non-conscious minds take things very literally, but they can be quite hard to override by our rational, conscious minds. For this reason, biometrics can give us another way to measure non-conscious responses in consumers.

After eye-tracking, biometric measures probably have the longest history of use in marketing research. As early as the 1960s advertising researchers were tracking measures such as skin conductance and heart rate, in a proto form of neuromarketing.

The nervous system

The key to understanding biometrics is to first understand a little of the organization of the human nervous system. The nervous system is organized into a number of subsystems (see Figure 9.1).

For our purposes, it is mainly the autonomic nervous system that we will be looking at. This system is involved with non-conscious regulation of our bodies. It is divided into the sympathetic and parasympathetic branches.

Overall, sympathetic nervous system activity is related to emotional arousal: it is the fight-or-flight system and is responsible for activities that require a quick response. The parasympathetic activity is often called the 'rest and digest' system. It is mainly responsible for the general bodily maintenance at rest activities, such as digestion, urination/defecation as well as sexual arousal.

FIGURE 9.1 The nested hierarchy organization of our nervous system

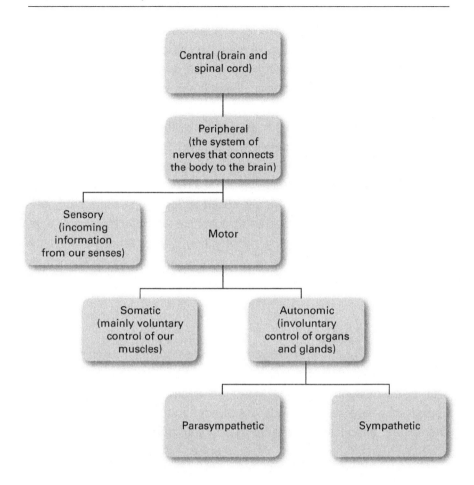

Key biometric considerations

One of the important considerations in biometric measurement is the law of initial values. This is that someone's biometric responsiveness at any moment of time will depend on his or her previous state. A simple example is that if you only had one number telling you a person's heart rate for one minute whilst they watched a TV ad break, it would be inconclusive on its own as you wouldn't know whether that person has a naturally high heart rate, has only just sat down after some form of exercise, or if it was purely their reaction to the TV ads that was accounting for that rate. One of the ways to minimize this effect is to take some initial baseline reading from the participant. Another is to look at ongoing changes, rather than the absolute values of a reading.

With heart activity and galvanic skin response (GSR) – perhaps the two most frequently used biometrics in market research – there are essentially two rhythms of activity. Tonic (sometimes called *level*) are the underlying, slower rhythms, whereas phasic (sometimes called *response*) is the temporary change caused by whatever we are currently reacting to. These are a little bit analogous to the tides (tonic) and the waves (phasic) on the sea. Analysing heart or GSR data needs to take both of these into account.

Another consideration with biometrics is to respect people's personal boundaries. As you are inviting people into a research location and asking them to undergo a slightly invasive procedure (putting sensors onto their body) it is important to keep the atmosphere as non-clinical and non-stressful as possible, whilst still conducting it in a structured way (to ensure that each participant goes through as identical an experience as possible, so as not to bias their reactions).

Heart activity

Roughly the size of our fist, our hearts pump somewhere between 3 and 4 billion times during our lives. Heart-rate sensors for health and fitness applications have become widespread now and usually either involve a chest strap that positions sensors against your skin, or optical sensors in a watch or wristband that can measure pulses of blood flow.

Whilst heart activity may seem like a poor relative to, for example, brain data, it contains a surprising amount of information. Readings of emotional arousal and attentional focus can be obtained from heart data. Broadly, when someone's focus is outward, their heart rate slows; when it is inward, it quickens.

The heart receives inputs from both the sympathetic and parasympathetic branches of the nervous system. Sympathetic activation speeds it up, parasympathetic slows it down. The two systems can work in tandem, opposite and independent of each other. The fact that our heart activity is driven by two systems slightly complicates matters, as a downward or upward movement in heart rate (for example) could be due to the activity in either system (see Table 9.1).

TABLE 9.1 Influences on heart rate

	Sympathetic Nervous System	Parasympathetic Nervous System
System activity increases	Heart faster	Heart slower
System activity decreases	Heart slower	Heart faster

One particular example of outward focus that shows up in the heart data is the orienting response. This occurs when something suddenly grabs our attention, such as someone calling our name, or if we see something novel or unexpected. This causes a slowing of the heart rate over a period of two to five heartbeats.

Conversely, concentrating on a more internal, mental task – such as performing some mental arithmetic, or carrying out a complex language task – has been shown to speed up our heart rate. Also, experiments have revealed that when people are shown highly emotionally unpleasant images their heart rates slow, and they quicken when shown highly positive images.

When watching TV ads, for example, heart rate may go up when there are changes of scene, or when the TV show ends and the ad break begins (akin to the orienting response), when there is something highly emotionally positive, or when there is something on screen that requires us to concentrate more. It can go down when we see something negative, or when we become bored and start thinking about something else.

There are essentially two ways to measure heart activity: by the electrical activity generated by the beating heart itself or by the pulse of blood flow created by the beating of the heart. The electrical measurement of heart activity is called an electrocardiogram (ECG or often EKG, after the German spelling) and is the more precise measure as it records the exact moment of each beat. However, ECG usually requires electrodes connected to the chest and is therefore a little more invasive to administer than measures of pulse, which can be obtained through wrist- or finger-band sensors. Measures of the time intervals inbetween beats is called heart rate variability, and is one of the most useful ways to measure heart activity.

Interestingly, a new method for measuring heart-rate changes via high-definition webcams is currently being tested. It works by detecting subtle variation in the colour of the skin, on a moment-by-moment basis that shows how fast the person's heart is pumping blood around the body. These changes in skin colouration are usually too subtle to be perceived by the human eye, but software can pick them up. It is too early to say how useful, reliable and valid this measure will be, but it does have the advantage of potentially working online, hence not incurring the greater expense of bringing participants into a central location.

Due to heart-monitoring sensors being comparatively cheap and small, they can in theory be used to make 'real-world' recordings from people (as long as they are combined with other measures and a way of correlating what the person was doing/looking at on a moment-by-moment basis), although obviously it is important to keep the person reasonably still, as the heart rate will go up with vigorous movement.

Heart-rate data is rarely used on its own in neuromarketing studies, but is sometimes used in combination with other metrics. By including other measures, or limiting the nature of the stimuli (either high/low attention, or positive/negative emotional content) of what you are showing participants can help disentangle the ambiguity of heart data.

Skin conductance (GSR or EDR)

Skin conductance is usually referred to as galvanic skin response (GSR) or sometimes electrodermal response (EDR). It is essentially used as a measure of emotional arousal and is controlled by the sympathetic nervous system.

There are two types of sweat glands: apocrine and eccrine. The former help to cool us down, whereas the latter are a lot more associated with psychological reactions. These glands are found in concentrated numbers on the palmar surfaces of your skin: the palms of your hands and the soles of your feet. The increased sweat production on the palms of the hands and soles of the feet has an evolutionary reason: it helped our hominid ancestors to grip things in times of danger when they had to quickly fight or flee. The palms of your hands may even become noticeably sweaty when you are nervous – this is essentially the same class of reaction that a GSR study measures, except for the fact that most stimuli under testing will not cause your palms to noticeably sweat, yet under the skin's surface the levels of sweat will have increased and this is enough to increase the electrical conductivity of the skin.

Most marketing studies that use GSR recordings do so from the hands. Two electrodes are placed on the person's non-dominant hand. You can either position them on the base of the thumb and the palm, or on the midpoint of two fingers.

However, it is also possible to measure from the soles of the feet and this may be necessary if it is essential that the person has both their hands unencumbered in order to use them to interact with something (too much movement of the hand can disrupt the signal on the sensors). In this case the sensors are placed on the underside of two toes.

GSR is perhaps most relevant to marketing studies where you want to measure the ongoing responses to emotional videos (such as ads, or videos showing experiences). In particular it may be most useful where you need to track the emotional response to longer videos, such as a whole TV show or movie. The signal is not as quick to respond as, for example, the electroencephalography (EEG) brain signal and can lag several seconds behind the stimulus. For this reason it does not always have the greatest use with short ads with fast cuts that may evoke lots of different levels of emotional response during a very short time. One type of response that GSR excels at is the more visceral emotional reactions that come from either highly emotive imagery or from watching things that may create in us a bodily empathy (eg watching extreme sports, where you begin to feel the bodily risks in sympathy with the person you are watching).

GSR recording is relatively easy to set up: putting on the sensors is fairly simple and, although the person needs to keep their non-dominant hand still, it is otherwise not very invasive.

The Swiss psychoanalyst Carl Jung was an early devotee of GSR as a window into the non-conscious mind. His patients would wear a GSR monitor whilst he asked them questions, to see if there were any notable non-conscious emotional responses to what was being said.

Pupillometry

Pupillometry measures changes in the pupil of the eye. Whilst the visual cortex in the brain controls decoding of what we see, it is the autonomic nervous system that controls the size of our pupils. Hence its inclusion in this biometric chapter rather than with eye-tracking, although in practice it is often measured by an eye-tracker.

The size of our pupils is controlled by two sets of muscles in the iris (the iris is the coloured part of your eye). One is a circular muscle set that works to constrict the pupil, the other is a series of radial bike-spoke-like muscles that expand the pupil. The former are under control of the parasympathetic nervous system, the latter the sympathetic. This results in a similar push/pull dual system effect, as in heart-rate activity.

Pupil diameter is affected by three main factors: light conditions, cognitive activity and emotional arousal or engagement. Cognitive load, as you will recall from Chapter 2, is the amount of mental effort that we have to put into a task. Habitual tasks such as tying a shoelace or making a cup of coffee will require a low load; mentally adding up the cost of your grocery shopping or filling in your tax form will place you under a heavier load. The greater the load, the more your pupils dilate (although, interestingly, no one yet understands why). In theory this makes pupil diameter a good measure of how much effort something is requiring. However, in practice, because the pupil diameter is also affected by changes in surrounding light levels, this is not a straightforward measure. This means that it is usually best to stick to testing still images, where there is a constant level of illumination, rather than moving videos with constantly changing illumination levels.

Daniel Kahneman conducted some pioneering experiments using pupillometry as a measure of cognitive load. 'The pupils reflect the extent of mental effort in an incredibly precise way,' he comments. 'I have never done any work in which the measurement is so precise.'[1] Pupillometry has been used extensively in psychological research and has even been shown to predict when someone is about to make a decision (albeit only a second before, in a simple button-pushing task).

However, even controlling for light conditions does not completely remove this problem as there are also irregular fluctuations in pupil size that occur, called the 'light reflex'. ICA (Index of Cognitive Activity) is a patented technique for measuring the cognitive-load aspect of pupil dilation. Rather than measuring the overall pupil size, it instead measures the rate of tiny, fast dilations – a measure that is not affected by changing light levels, therefore making it a more robust measure of cognitive activity. It uses a mathematical technique called wavelet analysis to separate out the two sources of pupil dilation. Light-related changes to the pupil's size tend to be comparatively slow and large and ICA simply goes through the data and filters out these changes. As well as being a purer measure of cognitive activity, ICA measures also move faster, making them a better second-by-second measure of cognitive activity.

Pupil dilation can also be a sign of interest or attraction. The measure was briefly in vogue in the 1970s in advertising research as a measure of our attraction to visual images of objects or people. Magicians have long known about this effect and during card tricks can carefully watch a person's eyes to identify when their chosen card turns up. Also, Chinese jade dealers used to watch prospective customers' eyes to figure out when there was enough interest to raise their prices.

Other measures

Whilst heart-rate measures and GSR are the most frequently used biometrics, there are several other measures that are also sometimes used, as given below.

Voice analysis

Emotional information is obviously contained within our voices and such sound patterns are amenable to automated computer analysis. Whilst not currently a mainstream neuromarketing method, an advantage of voice analysis is that it can be done online, or remotely, hence not requiring the additional overheads of lab-based studies.

Respiration rate

Our rate of breathing can be voluntary or involuntary and is highly correlated with heart rate. Outside clinical settings this can be measured with a chest strap. Emotional arousal can cause increases in respiration rate. In practice, however, this measure is rarely used in neuromarketing research.

Facial electromyography (fEMG)

As an alternative to automated facial coding, the activation of the facial muscles can be measured directly with sensors positioned on the face. Obviously this is more invasive and expensive than facial action coding via webcam.

Posture and movement

Movement data can be captured with multi-axial accelerometer sensors placed on the participant, or, as with voice analysis, posture has the advantage of being 'capture-able' remotely, via cameras such as web cameras whilst a person is watching a video online.

One of the ways that our brain treats emotions is in terms of whether we feel motivated to move towards or away from something: whether it is a threat or an opportunity. For example, if we are particularly interested in something we are looking at on our computer screen, we may physically lean in closer. As it can be captured by camera, this kind of postural movement can be incorporated into facial action coding or eye-tracking measures.

Physiology and sensory marketing

Whilst marketers are used to creating visuals, our other senses are often overlooked. Understanding our other senses can yield new insights into making brands more distinctive and memorable, and making products more enriching and pleasurable to use/consume. The effects of sensory marketing, or sensory aspects of products, are often non-conscious. For example, the atmospherics of a store (light levels, background music, temperature and scents present in the air and so on) will typically combine to influence our emotions or mood, without us being consciously aware of it.

There are priming effects with sensory perception. One obvious example is that seeing a delicious-looking meal can cause heightened appreciation of taste (increased saliva production also helps in breaking down the chemicals in the food in your mouth, enhancing taste). However, there are many other ways in which one sense can activate, enhance or change another. Temperature, vibration and weight can all alter our sense of touch, for example.

As brand managers and creatives think more about the non-conscious aspects of communication, understanding the physiology behind sensory reactions will become more important.

Wearables

Although most biometric studies have historically been conducted by bringing people into a central location, the lower cost of the equipment and even the proliferation of consumer devices that can measure biometrics are opening up the possibility for in-home studies.

One model is for the researcher to create a panel of people to whom they can mail out the sensors for them to use at home. Obviously this has cost implications and if the panel is to be used repeatedly there is the danger of them becoming too familiar with the testing formats and hence potentially reacting in ways different from the general population.

Another model that may become feasible in the near future is to use participants' own sensors. For example, as fitness monitoring devices such as smartwatches with heart-activity monitors become more popular, it may be possible to recruit enough people who own them to take part in research at home using their own equipment. In this case it would be important to know that the range of devices used are either the same make or not too dissimilar in accuracy, so that differences in results are not just due to differences in the equipment used. There would also need to be some way of time-synching the recording with the stimuli that the participants are being shown. Currently there are not any providers who have developed such systems but it may become possible in the near future.

CASE STUDY   Biometric measures of emotion from TV ads

Most TV ad creators know that music can be a powerful way to generate emotional engagement in an ad. Not only does music itself have powerful emotional qualities, but it can create these emotional effects quickly. Given that ads often have as little as 15–20 seconds to emotionally affect their audience, this ability can be very useful. Sensum, a UK-based full-service neuromarketing agency, conducted some exploratory research using GSR to study the effect of music in TV ads. Biometrics are ideal for this type of research question as they can measure emotional arousal in a relatively non-invasive way, meaning that the participants can sit back and watch TV as they normally would at home. The Sensum system uses a wristband GSR with finger sensors that synchs wirelessly to a tablet or laptop, where videos or images can be viewed, before the biometric data is then seamlessly uploaded for analysis.

Before measuring the ads themselves, Sensum conducted a pilot study to confirm the ability of the GSR equipment to accurately measure emotional reactions to sound. Twenty participants were played a series of previously standardized non-musical sounds and musical excerpts as well as being shown a series of images, all previously standardized as low or high in their emotional arousal effects.

Having confirmed that the GSR was accurately able to discriminate between the low and high arousal sounds and images, and also that the music created higher levels of arousal than the non-musical sounds, Sensum moved on to studying the ads themselves. This time, 33 participants were shown a series of 20 TV ads, in random order, embedded into ad breaks within a TV programme. The participants were organized into two groups: one group saw half of the ads with the music muted, the other group saw the same batch of ads but with the music muted on the opposite set of ads. The study also captured how previously aware or familiar the participants were with the ads.

In both studies the participants were screened using a breathing task to ensure that they were the type of person whose GSR is measurable. The GSR data was also cleaned to take out any artefact noise due to movement (any shifts of the device itself or excessive movements of the participants' fingers).

The results showed that when the ads contained music they were more emotionally arousing than those without music. There was no connection between familiarity and emotional arousal. This perhaps is unsurprising and confirms what you might expect. However, they were also able to find a correlation between the level of emotional arousal and the effectiveness of the ads. It was the presence of the music soundtrack that made the ads emotionally arousing.

'Audiovisual storytelling is at its best when it pushes our emotional buttons,' says Sensum's CEO and co-founder Gawain Morrison, 'and measuring the real-time physical responses to this ebb and flow can offer insights to greater creativity and more engaging content.'

Pros and cons of biometrics

The benefits of biometrics are that they can provide a moment-by-moment reading of a person's emotional responses and are (compared to the direct brain measures such as EEG and fMRI) comparatively cheap to run and easier to analyse.

They are also easy to combine with other measures; for example whilst a person's heart activity or skin conductance is being monitored they can also have their brain or facial emotion activity monitored, or be eye-tracked.

In theory, the smallness, portability and cheapness of biometric sensors mean they have the potential for being used in many real-world situations. In practice, the complexities of correlating such measures with what the person was doing and experiencing second by second, and of filtering out physiological changes that are simply due to physical movements, mean that so far this is only done within relatively narrow applications.

Another limitation of biometrics is that whilst they are good for showing the amount of emotional arousal, they are not usually able to measure the actual emotion itself. For this reason they are usually combined with some other measure, be it one of the neuroscience measures or some form of questionnaire or conscious response. A typical output of this is an intersection of two axes, the vertical showing levels of arousal (from biometric measures) and the horizontal showing emotional 'quality' or valence (usually from another measure, such as facial coding or questionnaire response – see Figure 9.2.) Responses are then plotted within this space.

FIGURE 9.2   Combining a measure of emotional arousal with emotional valence

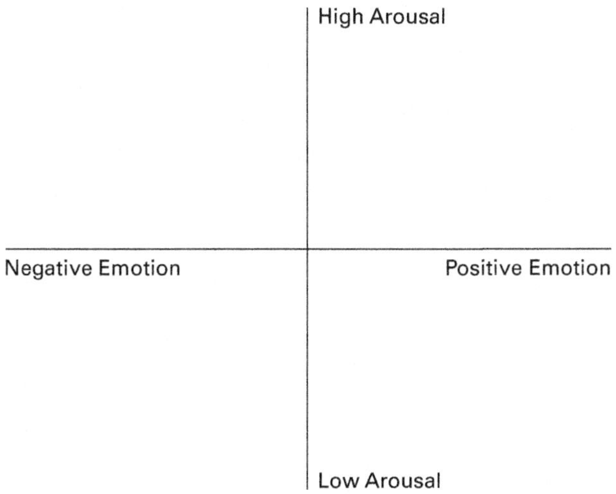

High Arousal

Negative Emotion | Positive Emotion

Low Arousal

Summary

- Biometrics are better at measuring the intensity of an emotion than its quality or type.
- Biometric signals are often inconclusive on their own, but more robust in combination.
- Heart activity can give an indication of a person's attention focus and emotional arousal.
- GSR – skin conductance – can give an indication of a person's emotional arousal.
- Pupillometry – measuring changes in the size of the eye's pupils – can give a measure of cognitive load, or difficulty of a task.

Note

1   Available [Online] http://www.spiegel.de/international/zeitgeist/interview-with-daniel-kahneman-on-the-pitfalls-of-intuition-and-memory-a-834407.html [accessed 24 April 2015].

NEURO-MEASURES 10

The techniques we have looked at so far all work through behavioural or bodily measures; in this chapter we look at direct measurements of brain activity. These measures tend to be more expensive and require more sophisticated and time-consuming analysis. Nevertheless, they are on an upward curve of techno-development, which in the years ahead can only see their speed and usability as well as their affordability increase. These measures also each have decades of prior research behind them, as well as being used extensively for marketing and advertising research, meaning that there is an ever-growing understanding of how they relate to consumer reactions.

Whilst there are numerous brain-recording techniques in existence, there are essentially three that are most suited to market research applications and are in regular use around the world today: functional magnetic resonance imaging (fMRI), electroencephalography (EEG) and steady state topography (SST). The first works by measuring blood flow through the brain; the other two measure patterns of rhythmic electrical activity emanating mainly from the top part of the brain: the cortex. Each has a limited window on brain activity: fMRI can image the whole brain, but comparatively slowly – thus missing faster activity – whilst EEG and SST are able to record activity at the millisecond level, yet cannot directly measure activity from the deeper parts of the brain.

Brain-recording technologies can seem like magic boxes that can read our minds, but this is not the right way to view them. Whilst these devices give us images of mental activity, they are not like cameras. A camera can be picked up and used even by a child, and will give you a meaningful picture (even if it doesn't look especially well composed). In contrast, the information gleaned from neuro-recordings is dependent on a good and appropriate experimental design being executed well by someone who knows how to use the equipment. Without this expertise, the data alone can be useless. For this reason (in addition to the extra costs, and the more sophisticated analysis required) these techniques are somewhat less accessible than the techniques in the preceding chapters, and hence it is more likely that you will need to rely more on a third-party supplier (although an increasing number of agencies are using EEG 'in-house'). Therefore, this chapter will focus on giving you enough information to understand the basics of the pros and cons of using these techniques for market research.

fMRI

Functional magnetic resonance imaging (fMRI; standard magnetic resonance imaging (MRI) without the 'f') is equivalent to taking still photos of the brain – the added 'f' is like taking movies of the brain during activity. Essentially, fMRI involves the participant lying inside a large chamber that creates magnetic fields, revealing the location of oxygen-rich and oxygen-poor blood in the brain. fMRI works on the principle that the more active an area is in the brain, the more energy it consumes, and the more it needs a flow of blood to replenish glucose and oxygen levels. A brain area works to perform a task, and two seconds later oxygen-rich blood floods in to re-energize it. It is this process that fMRI tracks.

fMRI scanners are expensive (millions of pounds) and require housing in a permanent location (most of them are in hospitals or university research centres). Commercial researchers will often 'rent time' on these scanners, rather than acquire their own.

The key strength of fMRI is its exceptional spatial resolution: the ability to record activity down to small areas of the brain, including the deeper, more evolutionarily primitive structures that can be involved in emotional experiencing, such as those that comprise the limbic system. This gives it the edge in being able to pinpoint direct activation of, for example, particular emotional states within the brain in a way that other methods cannot.

Some of the publicity attached to certain fMRI findings throughout the years has led to criticisms of oversimplification of the degree to which a particular mental function (such as an emotion) can be isolated to a particular brain structure. Whilst the popular understanding of the brain is often that a certain area 'lights up', it unequivocally means that a particular mental event is occurring; in reality, things are more complex. For example, particular brain structures are often implicated in numerous different functions, and just seeing them becoming active does not necessarily tell us which function is occurring. The brain is a networked system, with multiple areas operating together in tandem rather than discrete areas always sticking to their own tasks. Imagine looking at a satellite image of London, seeing it more brightly lit than other geographical areas and using our knowledge that London is one of the globe's key financial centres to conclude that there is a lot of banking occurring. Apart from the fact that the photo was taken at night, and therefore banking activities are likely to be reduced, there are many other activities that London will be engaged in that are nothing to do with banking. The point is that such simple conclusions are flawed. Good researchers will avoid falling into this trap, but it may be worth bearing in mind, so as not to accept some of the wilder claims.

fMRI's real Achilles heel, however, is its relatively poor time resolution. Like a Victorian-era photographer, fMRI takes each picture over the course of several seconds. This means that it can fail to pick up more transient activity, eg picking apart the reactions to a fast-cut TV ad. Instead, it gives readouts over longer epochs of time (eg several seconds) or over the experience as a whole (eg the whole TV ad). This is improving with technical advances, but for the moment these types of scans are better at providing information about reactions that can be summarized over at least several seconds.

Another weakness of fMRI is its user experience. Not only does the study participant have to keep very still for extended periods of time (this particularly applies to the head) but they are contained within what can feel like a fairly oppressive clinical environment, inside a machine that can feel claustrophobic to some. This problem can be somewhat mitigated by either carefully recruiting those who are least likely to be fazed by this, or first allowing them to practise the experience, or both. Some facilities have dummy scanners that look and feel real, which allow people to try out and get used to the experience.

Nevertheless, despite these limitations, fMRI has been the sine qua non of the cognitive neuroscience revolution, giving us an unparalleled ability to see where brain activity is occurring, in almost real time. Like the early days of air travel, its commercial use, whilst attention-grabbing, has so far been more limited to occasional use by those with the deepest pockets. However, with innovative companies applying themselves to making fMRI more commercially appealing by changing the way they structure their studies (eg holding regular omnibus studies that allow multiple clients to share scanner time and therefore costs), plus ongoing technical innovations, it is likely to become more widely used in the years ahead.

CASE STUDY   fMRI – predicting ad performance at the concept stage

Netherlands-based firm Neurensics created a model for predicting ad performance based on fMRI data, based on ads that had won Effies, a marketing industry award for successful ads. However, knowing whether an ad is going to be effective or not is far more valuable at the concept stage, before money has been invested in filming it.

With this in mind Makro, a retailer with stores across South America, commissioned Neurensics to test ads that were still just concepts. First, the Neurensic scientists took a selection of ads for which they already had benchmark fMRI and marketplace performance data – some that had been successful, some unsuccessful. These ads were then turned into moving storyboards and retested. The results showed almost identical patterns of response to the completed ads, providing evidence that testing at the storyboard stage can provide valid results.

The Makro storyboard performed below average on a number of features that make up Neurensic's model of success, and they were advised on a number of changes to make before filming the real ad. Finally, the finished real ad was tested and it scored better than the storyboard version.

This study suggests that testing a variety of storyboard concepts before filming an ad can be a smart and more efficient way to use fMRI testing.

EEG

EEG, or electroencephalography (literally: electrical brain graphing), measures patterns of electrical activity mainly emanating from the top part of the brain, the cortex.

The cortex is the most evolutionarily recent part of the brain and is composed of six thin layers that are scrunched up to fit as much surface area as possible within the tight space of our skulls, so that it resembles a walnut. The cortex is mainly responsible for cognitive functions such as decoding the patterns in sensory information (sight, hearing etc), memories and planning of action – things that we would consider the 'higher' functions of our brain. The brain regions underneath the cortex (often referred to as subcortical structures) are more involved in activities such as regulating breathing and bodily functions, as well as our emotions. Of particular relevance is the limbic system, which is closely involved with emotional processing. These subcortical structures are more evolutionarily ancient (for example, we share them with a larger number of animals than those which have a cortex). Sometimes the fact that our brains evolved in evolutionary stages leads some to describe a 'triune' model of the brain, saying that we have reptilian, mammalian and human components to our brains. This is an oversimplification, as it fails to take into account the fact that even the more ancient parts of our brains have continued to evolve and adapt, and also that different structures of the brain are intimately interconnected, sharing information back and forth.

As neurons in the cortex fire up, they create small electromagnetic fields, and when groups of millions of neurons are firing in synchrony (think of big crowds of people clapping together in a sports stadium), the electromagnetic fields can be picked up by sensors placed around the scalp. There is an international standard system (referred to as 10/20) for positioning these sensors so that results from a recording can be compared to previous ones. The signals are then fed to an electronic amplifier before being sent to a computer for recording and, ultimately, analysis.

The benefits of EEG are that it is comparatively cheap; the lower-end equipment can be bought for only £100, although more expensive caps are preferable. The kit usually comprises either a range of sensors that fit into a cap, and then plug into a separate amplifier, or an all-in-one wireless cap that already contains the sensors and amplifier, which sends the data via Bluetooth to a computer. The caps can be fitted and adjusted to obtain a good signal in anything from several minutes to around a quarter of an hour, depending on the particular kit and the experience of the operator. Market researchers sometimes worry that the very experience of wearing a cap will be uncomfortable, and therefore make the person's reactions unnatural. However, if the cap fits, the person usually soon forgets they are wearing it.

Another virtue of EEG for market research is the fast speed, which means it can be correlated with eye-tracking measures. This can be a particularly useful feature as it allows information not only on where participants were looking, but how they were reacting whilst looking there. This can help to answer questions such as which areas of a package design are most effective, which packages on-shelf are being looked at, and how people are reacting to them; and not only what people are focusing on in a TV ad from moment to moment, but how they are reacting. In reality, however, combining EEG data and eye-tracking measures may result in a coarser level of eye-tracking detail than if you were using this measure on its own. You need to be able to gather enough eye-tracking data points that correspond, at the same moment, to good EEG data points in order to draw real conclusions.

One of the biggest challenges with EEG is that other sources of electrical activity can bleed into the recording data, and need to be eliminated. The main problem human activities are eye movements and blinking (mainly affecting the frontal sensors) or muscle activity (eg jaw or brow tension, or head movements). External sources of 'noise' can come from electrical equipment such as electrical cables running near the participant, or any other sources of electrical noise in the room such as overhead air-conditioning units. An experienced operator can usually eliminate most of these sources.

There are several types of EEG recording and analysis that can be done, usually without needing separate equipment. Probably the main type of EEG recording in use in marketing studies is frequency analysis. Within the EEG signal there are numerous different frequency bands, like the different instruments playing in an orchestra, or the different wavelengths of light that make different colours. Using a mathematical technique called Fast Fourier Transform (within the analysis software), the analyst can see how much amplitude (or power) there was of each frequency at each sensor location. This allows them to compute standard metrics, which are typically based on this information. This type of recording and analysis can give an ongoing, moment-by-moment level of data, and each metric can be depicted visually as a line graph, with time in seconds along the bottom (X) axis, and some measure of intensity of the metric as the side (Y) axis.

One of the most frequently measured EEG metrics is attention. This has been one of the more researched areas in EEG neuroscience (although, as we saw in Chapter 2, high levels of conscious attention are probably not as important to the effectiveness of many types of commercial stimuli as people used to think). Another frequently used metric is that of emotional engagement. To give measurements of moment-by-moment specific emotional activation you would need to be able to measure brain structures below the cortex, deeper than EEG can reach. However, there is one type of emotional processing that is done in the frontal cortex. It relates to the aspect of emotions that motivates us to move. We are constantly scanning our environment for potential threats or opportunities and, whenever we see them, we are motivated to move towards or away from them. There are differences in patterns of brain activity in the frontal sensor positions that can show this approach versus avoidance response.

Event-related potential (ERP)

An ERP is a small signal that occurs in response to a specific stimulus: for example, a sound or a word. Unlike the standard frequency analysis, these are not ongoing measures, but one at a time. Typically, the signals they measure are so small that you have to repeat trials many times and then average your data together before they become apparent.

Coherence analysis

Coherence analysis is a special form of frequency analysis in which activity in different brain regions is compared, in order to reveal if different areas are acting in synchrony together.

SST

Steady state topography (SST) is technologically similar to EEG in that it is measuring electrical brain activity, but it has an added innovation. Whilst the person's electrical brain activity is being recorded (for example, while watching a TV ad or viewing a poster image on a screen) a headset introduces a dim flickering light. This light induces a corresponding frequency of brain activity (a little like a glass resonating in sympathy with a high-pitched noise). This in turn enables one to measure changes in the speed of neural information processing in various parts of the brain and hence the level of brain activity. When particular areas of the brain are activated by what they are seeing (eg the ad), you can measure this activity more accurately because you can see it as a deviation away from the flicker rhythm that you have set up.

This innovation not only allows for more refined measures of brain activity, but it is also less susceptible to the muscle and movement noise in the data than a standard EEG recording.

While developed as a scientific research tool and described in the peer-reviewed literature since 1990, SST commercial services are offered exclusively through the company 'Neuro-Insight' and its licensees (**www.neuro-insight.com**), and is therefore not a technology that one can buy and use 'off the shelf'. The measures that Neuro-Insight offer currently include visual attention, long-term memory encoding, personal engagement, motivational valence (approach versus withdrawal) and emotional intensity.

Summary

- Whilst there are numerous brain-recording technologies, there are three that are in practical use for neuromarketing: fMRI, EEG and SST.

- fMRI is typically the most expensive of the three and it cannot give results over short time periods, but it can image deeper into the brain and provide specific readings of different emotional states.

- EEG is a cheaper and less invasive experience for participants. It can monitor responses over short time periods, which enables it to be combined with eye-tracking, and to give moment-by-moment readings to videos. However, it cannot image as deeply into the brain as fMRI and, despite its apparent portability, it is plagued by 'noise' if the participant moves too much.

- SST is a specialized variant of EEG. It adds a peripheral dim light flicker to set up a baseline of activity within the brain that activity can be measured against. SST cannot be paired with eye-tracking, and is only available through Neuro-Insight, but it can be regarded as superior to regular EEG, particularly in its ability to make recordings without electrical noise from muscle movement.

PART THREE
PUTTING IT ALL TOGETHER

COMPUTATIONAL NEUROSCIENCE   11

An early fictional illustration of eye-tracking advertising research was featured in the 1981 thriller movie *Looker*. A group of people are shown watching TV commercials in a futuristic-looking lab, whilst their gaze patterns are being monitored. By calculating individuals' scan paths the computer then automatically moves the product image to a position on the screen where it stands the best chance of being seen. However, the scene then turns sinister as it is revealed that the company behind it have tried to create the ultimate advertising actresses by putting them through plastic surgery. Their plan initially works, with the post-op actresses producing higher 'visual impact' scores, yet as soon as they move, their scores drop. Just optimizing their appearance was not enough. Something they didn't predict – the movements of the actresses – also played a role in how the audience responded. Deciding to take things to the next level, the Machiavellian research company cut out the live actresses altogether, replacing them with digital actors, optimized for perfect visual appeal in both appearance and movement.

Whilst such ideas seemed futuristic in the early 1980s, they are now more timely as we contemplate what is possible through combining understanding of the science of visual appeal with the increasing graphical and data-crunching power of computers. In one sense, the dystopian world of *Looker* has already come to pass, with the faces and bodies of magazine models so routinely heavily Photoshopped that they may as well be digital creations. The underlying mathematics of facial beauty are fairly well understood: symmetry of facial features, probably due to it being a signifier of good genes, confers a look that is beautiful to the majority of people. Yet it results in a sterile and often inhuman standard of beauty. Once we are able to create equivalent models of attraction and emotional engagement in other realms – videos, packaging, websites – will this result in a shallow world of lookalike designs? Or will it be a cheap, available-to-all tool for optimizing the beauty and attraction of the commercial designs around us? Indeed, will it even be possible to hack the underlying mathematical models of beauty in other domains as it has with the human face?

The types of neuro-design practices described in Chapter 3 are intended as guidelines, for forming research hypotheses and for interpreting the results of research. The key point is that there is still research being done on real people. However, as data on people's responses to ads accumulates, and as our understanding of the brain improves, the next logical step is to take such best practices and instantiate them in predictive models. This is part of the broader field of computational neuroscience that aims to build software models of how our brains work. In the realm of consumer research this means software algorithms that can analyse videos and images and predict how people will respond to them. This is the world of big data meeting the world of consumer neuroscience. With ever-increasing computational power and people interacting ever more with computers to do their shopping and watch advertising, the drive to make people more 'machine readable' will undoubtedly grow, whether we like it or not.

One way in which this could happen is with biometric sensors, such as those that monitor heart activity. If devices such as smartwatches with heart-rate sensors are worn by enough people, it may be possible to link their reactions to their online activity, the things they see and the things they buy. Interestingly, if this scenario were to occur, it would potentially cut out the research companies altogether, as large web or tech companies would be better placed to harvest, crunch and model such data. As consumer neuroscience databases grow in size, and computers grow in power, it will become possible to create increasingly sophisticated models of real-world responses and behaviours.

Would this result in the ultimate predictive power: artificially intelligent software that can predict what you want to buy before you even consciously know yourself? Or would it be powerful yet only within limited domains? For example, the rules and patterns behind how to make a good movie trailer are probably a lot simpler than how to make a good movie. Yet algorithms are already influencing people-watch, with services like the personalized recommendation engines on Netflix and Amazon Prime and websites such as RottenTomatoes.com and Metacritic.com computing rating scores for movies based on aggregating the opinions of critics. Yet whilst sites like RottenTomatoes.com undoubtedly measure something real about a movie's quality, a great degree of nuance and subtlety is lost in the aggregation.[1] This is not to mention the fact that the assumptions of the algorithm filter bias towards some types of movie and against others.

However, such algorithms have always in a sense been with us, as designers, artists and architects have long intuitively understood the patterns behind what people find beautiful.

Predicting successful music and movies

Although not strictly equivalent to advertising, research data on popular music and movies is a good analogy as there is hard data going back decades on their commercial popularity. After facial beauty, one of the next areas in which researchers have made the most progress is in understanding the effectiveness of pop music.

For example, in one study, the brains of 27 teenagers were monitored by fMRI whilst they listened to a number of new pop-music tracks that they had not heard before and were then asked to rate on a 1 to 5 scale.[2] Several years later the researchers found significant correlations between the brain data and actual sales: the data could predict the performance of around 3 in 10 of the hit songs and 9 in 10 of the flops. Interestingly, the conscious rating scores of the teenagers did not predict the actual sales. The teenagers' brains intuitively knew whether a song would be a hit or not, even though they did not consciously know this.

Another team have gathered up four decades' worth of UK pop-music chart success data and correlated it against 20 features of the music itself, such as harmonic complexity, dance-ability and length.[3] This resulted in a formula that can predict with 60 per cent accuracy whether a song will be a hit (making it into the top five) or a miss (not able to enter the top 30). Of course, real-world sales are also affected by marketing and the fame of the artist, so it may never be possible to predict with 100 per cent accuracy the sales success of a track. Interestingly, though, they found that they needed to tweak the relative importance, or weightings, of different features of the music for different periods of time. Tastes obviously change over time: as the mood of an era changes people become interested in different things, and different generations develop their own tastes.

The example of pop-music prediction is revealing: even with lots of real-world data, the model is still limited and its weightings still need to be tweaked according to the moment in time. It may be better at prediction after the fact rather than in predicting what will be popular in the coming year.

Pop music may seem to some to be a simple matter to predict in terms of success, as compared to more complex media, but similar algorithmic progress has been made in the realm of movie success. London-based Epagognix uses algorithms to predict the likely box-office success of scripts for movie studios. First they created a structure for tagging movie scripts on a large number of qualities, not just the directors and stars that are likely to be attached to them, but various elements of the stories themselves. Then they use artificial intelligence software to learn from decades of data on actual movie success, constantly refining the system by testing it with new scripts. They claim that the success rate of their predictions is high enough to make the film studios invest in their services.

Surprisingly, their predictions are not all about the talent or marketing behind a film, as you might think. One film studio gave them the scripts of nine unreleased movies to analyse – without knowing the stars, director or marketing budget. They were way off on their predictions of three of them, but on the rest they correctly predicted whether the films would be profitable or not (something that not all the studio executives predicted correctly) and they were uncannily accurate on their predictions on some of them. An executive from the studio said: 'I was impressed by the things they thought mattered to a movie. They weren't the things that we typically give credit to. They cared about the venue and whether it was a love story and very specific things about the plot that they were convinced determined the outcome more than anything else. It felt very objective. And they could care less about whether the lead was Tom Cruise or Tom Jones.'[4]

In a sense, an algorithm like Epagognix's is just a more sophisticated version of a human expert, such as a Hollywood producer, who would usually evaluate scripts on the basis of their own knowledge, perhaps often non-consciously feeling a hunch about whether a particular script had especial potential or not, although not being able to articulate why. The artificial intelligence takes things a step further, precisely quantifying and then cross-correlating the effects of many more variables than a human mind can compute – and without being subject to personal biases.

Predicting where you will look

One area in which advertising research is already being addressed by algorithms is visual perception. Whereas the algorithms for predicting the popularity of music and movies are based on behaviour data (sales figures), these algorithms are built on actual neuroscience knowledge: our understanding of the visual cortex. In particular, they are able to predict the regions of an image that are most likely to 'pop out' or draw the eye, a feature known as visual saliency.

Visual saliency in-store

Denmark-based Neurons Inc have developed an algorithm that can predict which areas of an image will most draw people's visual attention. Based on neuroscience understanding of the visual system, Neurons Inc's 'Neurovision' is an online platform where clients can upload their still images or videos for a fast, automated analysis that gives several outputs:

1 Perhaps most importantly, like eye-tracking it gives a heat-map-style visual overlay on top of the original imagery, which highlights the

areas that are most likely to draw people's gaze. These are the areas high in 'visual saliency', the feature that attracts our attention in a bottom-up, quick manner, separate from our personal search goals. When they analyse a *Where's Wally* children's book illustration, for example, they find several areas of high saliency, but all far away from where Wally actually is. This is perhaps a sign that the artists intuitively understand how to draw people's eyes away from Wally's true location.

2 It also analyses the image for its visual complexity. A good way of understanding the complexity of an image is to imagine how hard it is to compress the image. For example, the .bmp image file format on computers typically takes up more memory space than the same image in the .jpg format. If you took a .bmp image on your computer and saved it as a .jpg image, a conversion takes place that will compress it to a smaller file size; however, the less complex the image, the smaller size to which it can be compressed. For example, images that contain lots of blank space are less complex and can be compressed to smaller files. If an image has high visual complexity then it may be a sign that there is a lot of competition for attention within the image.

Neurons Inc were asked to help a US-based home-improvement store chain to help understand why their customers were having difficulty in finding their way around their stores. They had a series of signs hanging from the ceilings to signpost to customers where things were. The signs were very clearly designed and easy to read. Yet customers were not finding their way around. Neurons Inc tested a series of videos shot in-store and ran them through their Neurovision algorithm. What they found was that whilst the signs themselves may have been designed to be clear, the visual complexity of the store was so great that shoppers' eyes were simply being diverted to too many other things and they missed the signs. Neurons Inc then experimented with some different image manipulations to the signs in Photoshop, retesting to see what effect they had. This resulted in a cost-effective suggested solution: rather than the expensive exercise of redesigning the signs, simply move some of the in-store lighting so that it shines on the signs, increasing their visual saliency. After several weeks the store managers reported less shopper confusion as people began to find their way around more easily.

The algorithm is a good complement to traditional eye-tracking for a couple of reasons. First, it allows you to know that it is the visual saliency of an image or part of an image that is drawing the eye, rather than top-down drivers. With traditional eye-tracking it could be either. So it's more diagnostic, particularly when used in combination with eye-tracking: allowing you to see which aspects of the image are naturally drawing the eye and what people are choosing to look at to meet their goals. Second, the fact that it is faster and less expensive to use than real eye-tracking allows for many more cycles of experimentation. Images can be recut or manipulated to see what effect it has on their saliency patterns.

The maths of beauty

Another potential use of computational neuroscience is in searching for the underlying patterns behind what we find beautiful or emotionally engaging. It is not clear to what extent this might be possible. 'Beauty is no quality in things themselves,' according to the Scottish philosopher David Hume. 'It exists merely in the mind which contemplates them; and each mind perceives a different beauty.'[5]

For many people, their intuition tells them that algorithms should not be able to predict things such as pop songs and movie box-office success, yet it appears (within some limits) that they can. This means that it is hard to say how far the underlying codes of our reactions might be hacked by artificial intelligence algorithms.

As the writer Arthur Koestler pointed out: 'The Twentieth-Century European regards with justified misgivings the "reduction" of the world around him, of his experiences and emotions, into a set of abstract formulae, deprived of colour, warmth, meaning and value. To the Pythagoreans, on the contrary, the mathematization of experience meant not an impoverishment, but enrichment. Numbers were sacred to them as the purest of ideas, disembodied and ethereal... Numbers are eternal whilst everything else is perishable: they are of the nature not of matter, but of mind.'[6]

Some examples of the hidden maths behind things that we find attractive include:

- Many successful product design formats – including credit cards, magazines, TV and computer screens, playing cards, pens and even doorways – conform to the proportions of the 'golden ratio'. Aston

Martin admits that its designers deliberately use the golden ratio in designing their luxury sports cars.

The golden ratio is a mathematical pattern found a lot in nature (hence, perhaps, our evolved tendency to find it beautiful) and is deliberately used by Renaissance artists to make their paintings more pleasing and harmonious. In its horizontal form the golden ratio may embody the most natural and easy scan path for us humans. With two eyes and an evolutionary history spent largely on the East Africa savannahs, a horizontal viewing scan is faster for us than a vertical one. The optimal shape for us to scan – be it an image or a section of text – may therefore be the golden rectangle – resulting in a greater feeling of 'processing fluency' (see Chapter 3).[7]

- The enduring popularity of the 'drip paintings' of Jackson Pollock may be due to their use of hidden mathematical patterns that we perhaps perceive non-consciously. Mathematical analysis of his paintings has revealed that they share patterns with fractals (based on the maths of chaos theory). Fractal patterns are ubiquitous in nature, evident in the form of trees, mountain ranges and leaf patterns, again, perhaps accounting for our predilection for them. Interestingly, researchers have found an optimal 'density' of fractal images (density refers to the complexity of the fractal image) that people find pleasing to look at – and Pollock's paintings happen to be at this optimal density.[8]

- Most people are familiar with the idea that music has mathematical patterns, but sound frequencies themselves can also create emotional effects in us. For example, infrasound – sound frequencies just below our conscious awareness – have been shown to increase heart rate and feelings of unease or 'chills'. This may have an evolutionary reason, as many natural disasters often produce infrasound frequencies (eg tidal waves, earthquakes and hurricanes). Some have claimed that the Nazis used infrasound at their rallies to whip up anger and strong feelings in the crowds, whilst the makers of the horror film *Paranormal Activity* claimed that they used infrasound to cause feelings of fear and unease in the audience.

Art or science?

Considering the 'neuro-rules' for design and communication begs the question: is commercial communication more an art or a science? Indeed, some might feel that we are heading for a neuro-driven future in which design is almost driven by algorithm. However, it is doubtful that things will or can go this far. The true power to create good designs and communication still rests with the creatives, and the role of understanding consumers' irrational non-conscious minds is just another source of information that makes up the craft of good marketing, just as understanding how to use Photoshop, or how to best photograph a product.

There are several reasons for this:

- The marketplace never stands still: as soon as someone hits upon very effective ideas to use in advertising, design or packaging, they usually get copied and hence cease to be a source of competitive advantage, or the consumers themselves habituate or tire of the ideas and they cease to be effective. Equally, advertising and designs need to cater to the current changing needs of a marketplace: the tactics that are successful now may not be successful in 10 years' time.

- The world is complex and often non-linear: whilst having design principles can be very useful, it is still the case that some of the best ideas are those that break all the rules. Myriad factors, such as a brand's history, the current cultural and economic climate and the activities of your brand's competitors all feed into how people react to your communications. Equally, many elements mix together in an ad or design, and that mixing can create unique and unpredictable reactions in consumers.

- Rules only take you so far: neuro-rules can predict the sorts of formats of communication that, all other things being equal, will tend to perform better, but it still requires human creativity to come up with designs and advertising concepts in the first place. A skilled creative person will draw upon their intuition for inspiration – by understanding the ways in which we can decode consumers' non-conscious and intuitive responses we can give the creatives extra insight.

None of this is to negate the power of neuro-principles, just to keep them in perspective!

What will be the role of computational neuroscience?

In one sense, most of the consumer neuroscience vendors already use something like algorithmic prediction. Rarely is raw data presented, there is usually some filtering and computation involved in presenting scores that are in theory predictive of real-world success. These computations involve various assumptions about what creates success. In essence, this is a model of brain activity.

There will be a broader demand to make human emotions and intentions 'machine readable' from outside the market research community. As people around the world interact more with computers to conduct their daily lives, understanding more about how people are responding, in real time, will be of practical importance as well as commercial value.

It is easy to foresee an important role for these techniques. First, there will be an increasing demand for models to explain the results of real research. Many of the outputs from consumer neuroscience research are ambiguous, without context and assumptions with which to interpret them. This obviously creates a demand for large and intelligently con-structed databases from which to draw comparison benchmarks. It also means that we will need a greater understanding of the decision-making process. Currently there is no dominant, accepted universal model of how consumers make decisions: merely a myriad of competing theories and localized models that have been refined to explain one particular aspect of consumer decision-making.

Another way in which algorithms can be helpful is as an analysis tool. Up until now many aspects of putting together a consumer neuroscience report have been somewhat laborious. Some vendors have succeeded in automating reporting to a degree, but as the analyst works his or her way through the data, deciding what it is showing, they will have need to create new graphs, or to interrogate the existing graphs in different ways that the basic automation could not have predicted. Intelligent algorithms could provide tools that help analysts. For example, algorithms could analyse any videos being studied and overlay them with tags that describe their features. An analyst may find it useful to have an automated series of marks placed on the timeline of an ad showing cuts, scene changes, sound levels, brightness, visual complexity and so on. These features could be useful in understanding the bottom-up reactions in the data to what is being seen on-screen. For example, we know that lots of fast cutting will tend to increase attention. Knowing where the cuts are, or positions of scene changes, could speed up the analyst's job of understanding the flow of viewers' attention. Similarly, such algorithms could be used to do a first-pass analysis of the data. They could look for correlations between the ads that were studied and the reactions to them, and compare for similar reactions to similar visual features in the database. When the human analyst sits down to look at the data, they would then already have a series of suggested hypotheses for the results. Maybe the algorithm would find that in 70 per cent of previous ads that have used the same camera movement as the current ad, they also saw a surge in emotional intensity of the viewers: hypothesis – this camera movement is emotionally engaging. It is then up to the human analyst to decide if the hypothesis makes sense or not. Whilst (currently) such algorithms are getting good at analysing the bottom-up visual and sound features of an ad, they are not so good at understanding meaning and context, the top-down features. Just as someone from one culture may miss the nuance or humour present in an ad from another culture, computers are not currently adept at understanding that side of life.

With the ever-increasing power of machine learning it seems inevitable that these types of models and algorithms will grow in use in the future. Real research, with real people, can be comparatively expensive and time-consuming. There will always be a temptation to cut out the need for this research if there appears to be a quicker, cheaper alternative. Yet the real power of computational neuroscience is in tandem with real research.

Summary

- As we learn more about how people respond to images and videos, and as computers increase in power, there is the possibility of developing software models to predict responses. The field that deals with modelling the brain in this way is called computational neuroscience.

- There are already computational models that can predict the success of pop music and commercial movies.

- Software is commercially available for marketers and designers to analyse the 'visual saliency' of an image or video. This gives information on which regions of the image are likely to be attractive to our visual systems and how complex an image is (giving an indication of how hard it will be for people to process it).

- There is a long history of decoding the beauty or attractiveness of images and designs using mathematical concepts.

- Rather than replace designers, computational neuroscience will likely become a useful tool for them, providing insights into how people will likely respond to images and videos.

Notes

1 Similar to the 'wisdom of crowds' method (See Chapter 12), these review aggregator sites measure degree of consensus rather than level of quality, or strength of reaction per se. It is possible, for example, that a film for which half the critics felt passionately moved by it could receive a lower score than a film in which three-quarters felt the film was just 'okay' but none felt passionate about it.

2 Berns, GS and Moore, E (2012) A neural predictor of cultural popularity, *Journal of Consumer Psychology*, **22**, pp 154–62.

3 Available [Online] http://www.wired.com/2011/12/hit-potential-equation/ [accessed 24 April 2015].

4 Gladwell, M (2006) [accessed 24 April 2015] The Formula, *The New Yorker* [Online] http://www.newyorker.com/magazine/2006/10/16/the-formula.

5 Hume, D (1987) *Essays, Moral, Political and Literary*, 2nd edn, Liberty Fund, London.

6 Koestler, A (1959) *The Sleepwalkers*, Penguin, London.

7 However, more recent research (such as: Stieger, S and Viren, S (2015) Time to let go? No automatic aesthetic preference for the Golden Ratio in art pictures, *Psychology of Aesthetics, Creativity and the Arts*, **9** (1), pp 91–100) suggests that this preference is not universal. The fact that it was used in ancient architecture and medieval painting may have been driven more by philosophical and religious beliefs that certain mathematical proportions should be naturally beautiful.

8 Jones-Smith, K and Mathur, H (2006) Fractal analysis: revisiting Pollock's drip paintings, *Nature*, **444**, pp E9–E10.

SMARTER SURVEY DESIGN

As we have seen earlier in the book, consumers are limited in their ability to verbally express the underlying attitudes and motivations that are driving their behaviour. Nevertheless, questionnaires are still a popular method for surveying consumers' attitudes. They can be cheap, quick and easy to administer, and can be tailored to address the exact research questions at hand. They are great for capturing the sorts of things consumers are saying to one another about a brand, product or service (the 'buzz'). They can also uncover objections that might be scuppering communications that work well at the non-conscious level (eg a product that has appealing communications but is just too expensive for consumers). Questionnaire results can also be useful to compare and contrast with non-conscious measures. However, even when asking questions it is important to bear in mind that the answers will usually reflect a mix of both system 1 and system 2 thinking, as our intuitive minds feed our conscious minds with information or preferences.

Psychological limits to survey design

To expand on the points made in Chapter 1, there are several basic limitations of consciously questioning consumers:

- lack of insight;
- memory limits;
- need for consistency;
- social desirability.

These are explored in more detail below.

Lack of insight

As we saw earlier, consumers often do not have introspective access to the non-conscious processes and associations that are driving their decisions. Yet instead of admitting to themselves or the questionnaire that they don't know, they are more likely to unwittingly fabricate a plausible-sounding answer.

Survey implication

Don't push too hard on questions that ask consumers things that they might not have genuine insight into. These are usually questions asking them to explain their motivations for buying something. If you do ask these questions, consider either asking them in a more indirect way (see more on this later in the chapter) or at least be aware of the tendency of consumers to fabricate plausible-sounding but incorrect explanations when they do not have introspective access to why they really bought something.

Memory limits

We have already seen, for example, that people's memories of emotional experiences tend to be different from the experience itself, and instead computed from the 'peak' and 'end' moments. Therefore, asking people to recall how something felt may give you a different answer than how it actually felt (although the memory alone can be useful, as it is what people will refer back to when they decide whether to do the thing again). We all have a limited memory, and tend to reconstruct our memories rather than access them in a pristine and accurate form.

Another of these biases of memory is misattribution. For example, sometimes we recall something someone said but think that someone else said it.

Survey implication

Keep in mind that consumers' memories are imperfect. Recall is harder than recognition.

Need for consistency

Imagine you are walking down the street and suddenly realize you are going in the wrong direction. As you turn around, do you first stop and pretend to check your phone or otherwise act out some observable behavioural reason for turning on your heels and suddenly going in the opposite direction? Many of us do, as we don't like to appear inconsistent to others or ourselves. One of the purposes of consciously rationalizing our behaviour is to smooth out such inconsistencies.

Survey implication

Be mindful of asking 'why?' questions, as they will often yield an apparently inconsistent, irrational aspect to consumers' behaviour that they will feel the need to hide or rationalize.

Social desirability

There are many areas in which consumers may try to hide their true attitudes, including behaviours that may be deemed bad (eg smoking or indulgent eating), that may make the person appear prejudiced (eg their preference for brands from their own country versus foreign brands), or behaviours that may make the person seem unintelligent (eg purchasing items that are unsophisticated or that are not good value for money).

Survey implication

Reassure respondents of the anonymous nature of the survey and/or phrase the possible answers in a way that makes each sound an acceptable choice (obviously whilst taking care not to lead them).

Theory of planned behaviour

Many attitude measures are weak at predicting actual behaviour. The theory of planned behaviour was developed in the 1980s by psychologist Icek Ajzen, and aims to explain the link between attitudes and behaviour. Studies seem to show that this model is good at predicting actual behaviour. It is based around three elements that combine to create a person's intent to act in a particular way:

1 The person's attitude towards a specific behaviour (including how often they have done it in the past).

2 What they see as the normal attitudes of others towards that behaviour.

3 Things that may limit their own behaviour.

For example, if we take the behaviour of buying a particular food product, we might ask the person buying it whether they think it tastes good and how often they have bought it before (their own attitude), whether they think their friends and family like and buy it (the normal behaviours of their peer group), and if it is affordable and they think they will actually get opportunities to cook and eat it (things that might constrain their behaviour). We may hold a positive attitude towards a product, but if we are surrounded by people who don't want us to buy it, or it is not affordable for us, we probably won't buy it.

The theory itself is most directly relevant to behaviours that we plan or intend to carry out. For example, it may be particularly relevant to people's intentions to buy a completely new type of product or service (such as adopting a new technology) or make a major purchase that requires deliberation (such as a new car or computer).

In contrast, much of the purchasing behaviour that this book is focused on is more perceptual and non-conscious processing influences on how consumers perceive ads and commercial communications. Nevertheless, it does have some good practical ideas that can be applied to improve questionnaire design. For example:

- Instead of asking how much the person likes a product or service, ask them how often they use it.

- Ask what might stop them buying or consuming it.

- Ask them how often they would have opportunities to buy or use it.

- Ask what they think other people like them think of the product or service, or whether their friends and family would approve of them buying it.

It can be easier for people to report how often they have bought something than to ask them to describe how they feel about it. Often people don't like to admit that they might be influenced by marketing communications. If you take the focus off them and ask instead about how they think others feel about it, you can get more accurate answers.

Cognitive interviewing

One of the ways to minimize the above problems when drafting a questionnaire is to first do a test version. This could be given to colleagues for proofreading, as often a fresh pair of eyes will spot potential weaknesses. It can also be trialled on your target market themselves. However, testing alone may not reveal any of the problems that your questionnaire might have. A technique for test-running a questionnaire in a way that can systematically search for such problems is called cognitive interviewing. Its aim is to generate understanding of how respondents are interpreting your questions. It uses techniques such as: 1) asking respondents to rephrase your questions in order to check their understanding; 2) asking respondents to explain what particular words or phrases used in the questionnaire mean to them.

Terms such as quality, healthy, green or nutritious, used frequently in marketing communications, can connote different things to different people. The fact that respondents may not always have introspective access to their own thinking, or may not want to report it, is a fundamental limitation of questionnaires. Yet there is another problem that we can do something about: respondents simply not correctly understanding the questions you are asking them.

In real-life conversations it is rare for people to ask the same question more than once. If the answer is not what they were looking for, the person can instantly follow up with a *different* question that clarifies what they really wanted to know, whereas surveys often have to make do with repeating the same question, just using a different phrasing. Such dynamic and interactive features of everyday questioning keep the trains of conversation on the right tracks, heading in the desired direction. In contrast, questionnaires rarely allow for the ability to clarify the meaning of a question (unless they are being administered in person, and even then some questioners will not have standardized definitions or explanations to give).

Cognitive interviewing can give flashes of insight into how your target consumers are interpreting your questions, and how they think about the product or service category. Obviously cognitive interviewing – or any pre-testing – relies upon having the luxury of time and resources. Although a cognitive interview test with as few as 10 respondents can be useful, the more respondents the better, and conducting more than one iteration of tests is also preferable.

Measuring the wisdom of crowds

Some find it hard to believe, but asking a crowd of non-experts to predict the outcome or success of something, such as the box-office receipts of a forthcoming movie, can be surprisingly effective.

The effect probably works by pulling in a diversity of opinions and sources of information. It increases the chances that various pieces of pertinent information that not everyone might be aware of are feeding into the decision-making, reducing the chances of something being overlooked.

The 'wisdom of crowds' effect only works when the answers given by each person are independent. For example, it is not the same as a focus group, where each person is able to hear the answers that others are giving, and are therefore potentially being affected by them.

Media Predict (**http://www.mediapredict.com**) offers an online 'wisdom of crowds' inspired service that aims to predict the success of new movies. The site is a betting market, where people can sign up, pay $10 into their betting account then choose questions on which to bet on the outcome. Each question has some kind of indication of the current market prediction, so that respondents have some expectation to consider and react against.

Prediction markets seem to work best when several conditions are in place. First, when the sample is self-selecting. In a standard survey those who are best placed to give answers (ie who may have more self-insight into how/why they buy a product, or who are just more articulate) get mixed in together with those who are less able, and there is no way of separating the two. However, in a good prediction market test, respondents are selecting themselves on their confidence of being able to answer the question accurately. Second, that the respondents are independent: they are not hearing the rationales of others as to how they are betting.

The sample size is, interestingly, somewhat determined by the consistency of opinion amongst those who enter. Eventually the spread of responses begins to stabilize and, when a level of equilibrium is reached, the betting is stopped.

Creating smarter surveys

Pre-test for order priming

In one study, university students were asked to rate their feelings of satisfaction with life, and then asked how many dates they had been on in the past month. There was no correlation between the two. However, in a second condition when they were instead first asked how many dates they had been on, and then asked to rate their satisfaction with life, there was a correlation. The very act of asking the first question had primed them to react differently to the second question. For this reason it can be important to think whether or not the order of your questions might be priming respondents in this way.

Sense-check your survey to make sure that there are no questions early on that suggest lines of thought that could bias respondents' answers to questions later on.

Frame questions indirectly

Similarly, sometimes people discount their feelings when answering attitude-type questions. By asking them what their 'gut feelings' are towards a brand or piece of communication, you can get more system 1/ implicit-like answers.[1]

General positive or negative orientation towards a brand or product can be inferred by asking indirect questions. One form of indirect questioning is projective tests. For example, the inkblot-type tests that came out of psychoanalysis, and were designed to reveal something about the person's personality. Indirect measures of attitude fell out of fashion in the 1970s and 1980s. Then the area saw an upswing of interest in the 1990s with the development of the idea of implicit attitudes (see Chapter 7).

One particular projective questioning technique that can be useful for surveys is the error choice technique.

The error choice technique

First described in a research paper published in 1948, the technique is based upon the idea that when people are forced to guess the answer to a factual question, their guesses will not be random but will instead be systematically influenced by their attitudes.[2] Because the questions are apparently factual, people are not alerted to it being an attitude test.

In a study conducted in the mid-1950s, students from two US universities watched the same film of a football match between their two teams. Students were more likely to see examples of unfairness in the opposing team: their attitudes biased their perception.[3]

In the original 1948 study the error choice questions were multiple choice, with two possible answers. As the respondents wouldn't know the correct answer, they were forced to guess, and one of the possible answers was at least slightly insulting or negative, the other flattering or positive. These questions were interspersed with factual questions that had more of a determinate answer, and one that did not imply a positive or negative attitude. The presence of these filler questions was to help mask the true intent of the questionnaire. The paper's author recommended that filler questions should outnumber the error choice questions by two to one, and that there should be four possible answers to each error choice question.

Here are some example error choice questions about a hypothetical brand:

- What percentage of its net profits does brand X donate to charity?
  – (a) 0.01 per cent, (b) 0.02 per cent, (c) 5 per cent, (d) 8 per cent.

- In an official evaluation of how green/environmentally friendly brand X's factories are, what do you think their score was?

- What percentage of users of brand X are university educated?

Note that direct measures of attitude may sometimes merely reflect 'public face' attitudes we hold; indirect measures may instead tap into underlying attitudes that are more predictive of actual behaviour. Hence the two may not correlate well.

Scales affect answers

Similar to the 'choice architecture' effects mentioned in Chapter 4, the options that people are presented with can affect the way they choose. In particular, respondents can become 'anchored' by the choice of a scale that you give them.

There is also some evidence of cultural variation in how people use scales, with some cultures more open to giving more extreme scores than others, making it difficult to directly compare results across cultures.

Central tendency bias: respondents are drawn more towards mid-range scores and less towards the outer extremes of a scale. Also, the midpoint of a scale – even if labelled as 'neutral' (eg 'neither agree nor disagree') tends to become the default answer for respondents who don't really know or don't want to give their true response.

Measure relevance of questions

Often questions are posed in such a way that respondents are forced to think in ways in which they wouldn't normally, resulting in artificial answers. Equally, probing too hard with explicit questioning about feelings towards something like a brand can just trigger guesses, or respondents might just parrot back to you slogans or advertising communications that they can recall. Most consumers do not consciously think too often or hard about the range of feelings or emotions that they connect to a brand.

Design questions to be friction-free

Often questionnaires are boring for respondents, which may mean that they give up before completing them, or it may just be that their motivation drops off and they become less focused on the questions.

One of the ways in which this can be avoided is through 'gamification': using elements from games (such as tracking progress, or use of appealing graphics and sound) to make participants enjoy the experience more and keep them motivated to finish the questionnaire. This is particularly relevant for long questionnaires or those that otherwise feel effortful to complete. There is a sense of having to really focus your mind to do it, with little pleasure in return (other than, perhaps, the monetary incentive you are being given for participation).

The same applies for other areas where you might be asking consumers questions, such as sign-up or order forms. A good example of how one website made a sign-up form more friction-free is the podcast-creation website Huffduffer (**http://www.huffduffer.com**). Rather than the typical sign-up form with drop-down menus that you have to scroll through to find your year of birth, or multiple boxes scattered around the screen with each asking something different, in a way that can feel unnatural and user-unfriendly, instead Huffduffer used this:

I would like to use Huffduffer. I want my username to be .... and

I want my password to be .... My email address is ....

By the way, my name is .... and my website is

....

This format of form succeeds in a couple of ways. First, it is more human, both in the language it uses and the format (actual sentences rather than separate 'commands' that request each bit of information). This makes it feel more familiar (and hence we have to think about it less) but also more friendly (it is more like a conversation, less like a curt interaction with a customs border guard!).

Second, it feels like an invitation to express yourself, to introduce yourself, which is inviting, as it feels more like a connection with a person than the typical web form, which feels like you are just populating cells in a computer database.

Ask for faster responses

By asking respondents to answer quickly, they have less scope for conscious deliberation and are less likely to confabulate plausible-sounding but spurious rationalizations. However it should be noted that this will not result in pure system 1 responses, but merely minimize some of the drawbacks of too much system 2 deliberation.

Ask questions in context

Often consumers will find it easier to answer questions about a particular behaviour (eg shopping) when they are in that mindset already. It aids their memory. Therefore, it can be preferable to ask your questions as close as possible to the time and place of the behaviour you are interested in. For example, if you are interested in supermarket-shopping behaviour it might be best to administer the survey in or just outside the supermarket (which, historically, has been done often). However, if it is not possible to physically administer a survey in a particular context, you can try to get as close as possible to it in time or ask people to imagine they are in that context when answering the questions.

Summary

- Traditional questionnaire designs may be improved by taking into account some of the limitations that consumers have in reporting their own reactions.

- A range of biases limit the things that consumers can report on, including biases of memory, limits of self-insight, the need to be self-consistent and the limits of attitudes in predicting behaviour.

- The theory of planned behaviour can be a useful framework for devising questions that will be predictive of actual behaviour.

- Cognitive interviewing techniques can provide a smart way to test-run a survey and understand better how the respondents might be misunderstanding or misinterpreting your questions.

- There are eight steps that you can use to help improve the quality of your surveys: pre-test, keep questions concrete, frame questions indirectly, be aware that scales can affect answers, measure the relevance of questions, design questions to be friction-free, ask for faster responses, and ask questions in context.

Notes

1 Ranganath, KA, Smith, CT and Nosek, BA (2008) Distinguishing automatic and controlled components of attitudes from direct and indirect measurement methods, *Journal of Experimental Social Psychology*, **44**, pp 386–96.

2 Hammon, KR (1948) Measuring attitudes by error-choice: an indirect method, *Journal of Abnormal Psychology*, **43** (1), pp 38–48.

3 Hastorf, AH and Cantril, H (1954) They saw a game: a case study, *Journal of Abnormal and Social Psychology*, **49** (1), pp 129–34.

COMBINING TECHNIQUES

13

The research methods covered in this book can each add something to our understanding of the irrational consumer. However, each of them only provides a limited channel of measurement. These are unlike the traditional use of questionnaires, which may be problematic in their ability to get at non-conscious thinking, but are certainly versatile. You can design a questionnaire to address any of your research questions. However, often within one research project one method may not be ideal for addressing all your questions. In theory, the intelligent and careful combination of methods should yield more robust and broader results. In practice, this can be difficult and full of potential pitfalls. In this chapter we cover some of the things to consider in combining techniques.

Due to the fact that online metrics are increasingly automated to set up, run and analyse, with a corresponding downward pressure on costs, adding multiple metrics into one online test often means only marginal extra expense, particularly if the same vendor offers the different metrics. In contrast, sometimes adding new metrics (eg biometrics or neuro-methods) can turn a test from being exclusively online, to needing a lab-based component, with the corresponding extra costs. So the rule of thumb is that adding more online methods together, or lab-based methods together, usually has minimal extra cost, but adding a lab-based method on to an online study will usually substantially increase costs.

However, one instance in which it makes sense to add lab-based research into an online study is running a pilot test. Often you can be more certain of the quality of data capture in the lab. As already mentioned (see Chapter 5) this is because you have the ability to directly monitor participants and to answer any questions they have in real time. You can also ensure that you have provided the best possible environment for testing, free of distractions, in a way that is not feasible using online testing.

Some typical combinations

Most of the methods covered in this book are combinable with the other methods. In general there are very few technical barriers (in theory) to combining any of the measures. The exceptions to this are fMRI and SST. The physical equipment used for these two metrics constrains what you can combine them with. For example, the SST headset is not practical to use at the same time as an eye-tracker, and the strong electromagnetic field of fMRI scanners makes it challenging to the point of impracticality to use with EEG (although it is possible that future technology developments will ease this problem).

There are essentially two types of combinations, which could be called tracking and parallel. Tracking combinations are where both methods are simultaneously tracking, moment by moment, an ad, video, audio or experience. They give outputs that are represented by either a line graph or video reply. Typically these would be used together for a richer understanding of a video or controlled experience, such as a structured web-usability task. In contrast, a parallel combination might include one tracking, moment-by-moment metric (such as EEG) with a metric that provides an overall score for the experience (such as implicit response measures).

Tracking combinations

Some of the most frequently used examples are given below.

Eye-tracking combinations

Eye-tracking is probably the most frequently combined metric. It often makes sense to combine eye-tracking with other measures as the gaze patterns show where people were looking whilst other measures can show how they were responding (thinking or feeling). Also it is relatively unobtrusive, so does not get in the way of any additional measures. For example, eye-tracking can be done with minimal experimental design: as long as the person's eyes have been calibrated, they have no further tasks or instructions to follow other than just looking at the images or videos.

Eye-tracking + EEG

In theory this can be a good combination on still images as you can use the eye-tracking measure to be more specific about how people are reacting to each area of the image. The restriction with this is that unless you use a very large sample, your eye-tracking 'hot zones' will be larger and therefore less specific than with regular eye-tracking. This is because you need to find a consensus of both regions viewed and reaction to that region. Nevertheless, this can be very useful, particularly when trying to tease apart reactions to the parts of an image, such as the broad regions of a pack design.

Eye-tracking + FAC

Similarly to combining with EEG, eye-tracking + facial coding can provide an idea of what people were looking at and how they were responding. In practice, however, the problem of needing a large sample is probably worse here as FAC readings only tend to give a response from a minority of participants at any given moment in time. Therefore, trying to find enough data for regions where the same people were looking, whilst also giving a detectable facial expression, may just be too difficult.

As well as tracking measures in combination with eye-tracking, it also makes a good complementary measure to use in parallel. For example, some of your research stimuli can be studied with one method, whilst other related material is eye-tracked. This might be useful where the budget is limited and you cannot afford to use both methods on everything.

Biometric combinations

Biometric combinations (eg heart activity + GSR) often make sense as such measures can become more robust or conclusive when used together.

Parallel combinations

These are combinations where you either run two separate yet complementary tests, or you have one test but with one metric giving you a moment-by-moment result and another giving you an overall summary result. A frequently used example is implicit response measures.

Combining implicit response measures

Implicit tests are generally designed to give an 'overall' reading of a piece of stimuli, rather than a moment-by-moment measure. However, there is generally no reason why the two cannot be combined. The implicit testing is done after and/or before the presentation of the stimuli, whilst the tracking measure (such as eye-tracking) occurs when the stimuli are being shown.

Implicit measures may give a better 'overall' reading of an ad than an average or computed score derived from a second-by-second metric. This is because the implicit score is genuinely the overall priming effect of an ad, whereas the computed average may be misleading.

Combining with questionnaire results

Selective use of explicit questioning can add value to a neuroscience study, providing extra context within which to analyse the results. The question that clients always ask is how to resolve a conflict between the non-conscious and explicit results. There is currently no agreed-upon framework for this, other than just to use common sense. If, for example, the neuro-results are positive, but the questions reveal negative responses, it may mean that there is something other than the perceptual aspects of the ad that the person objects to, such as the price of the product, or that they feel it is socially undesirable to feel positive about that product or ad. Alternatively, if they answer questions about an ad positively, but their neuro results reveal ambivalence or negativity, it could be that they are trying to appear socially acceptable by answering positively about this product or brand, or that they are still positive about it in spite of not liking that particular ad.

Another technique that is sometimes combined with neuroscience measures is a form of expert checklist completion. These usually involve a checklist of desired qualities that, for example, an ideal ad or design should have if it is to meet some minimum standard. Someone trained in understanding the checklist then evaluates the ad or design against it.

Eye-tracking + visual saliency

The visual saliency algorithm analysis mentioned in Chapter 11 is useful to combine with eye-tracking. Visual saliency shows which elements of an image are likely to draw attention just based on their raw visual features, whereas eye-tracking shows where people are actually looking. Where people will actually look is based not just on the raw details of the image, but the meaning of various details within it to people, and their goals for what they want to find in the image. Comparing the two sources of information can be instructive on which elements are 'popping out' just because of low-level visual features (such as contrasts and colours), and which are because people find them interesting at a higher level.

Visualizing combined results

One of the best and most intuitively user-friendly ways to combine results is in a video-playback dashboard. This is particularly useful for the moment-by-moment metrics, as their evolution over the time course of an ad can be synched. Typically, such dashboards are divided into several windows, one of which will show the video playback itself, whilst others are displaying the in-synch movement of each metric. They can also be useful for quickly switching between different cuts of the data. For example, displaying all the data by age group or gender is often achieved with just one click in a dashboard.

Anatomy of an ad

One way in which combining the results of different techniques can be useful is to understand what makes up a good ad. Each technique can add something to our understanding of this; combining them can give us a fuller picture.

For example, with print ads, such as those in magazines, eye-tracking, visual saliency and implicit response measures can give a fuller picture of how different versions will perform. Firstly, eye-tracking data can give useful information on which pages and areas in a page in the magazine are likely to be looked at most, for the more efficient use of the ad spend. Secondly, by running a visual saliency analysis of each version of the ad image, you can see which one is most likely to grab attention on the page. Magazine readers don't even look at all ads, so even just grabbing their initial attention is important. Thirdly, getting participants to look at each ad whilst they are eye-tracked will show which areas of the images and text get looked at first and in what order. This will reveal which version of the ad helps communicate the most important information first. For example, the most emotionally engaging part of the imagery, or the headline. Lastly, running implicit response tests after people have seen each ad image will show the concepts and ideas evoked by each one. Taken together these results will either reveal a clear winner, or will show which versions have the best strengths that could be combined into an improved version.

Combining measures is also useful with videos and TV ads. For example, measures like EEG, SST, eye-tracking, FAC and biometrics can give moment-by-moment results through the time course of the ad, whilst implicit response measures give a measure for the ad as a whole. This enables the analyst to see where the ad is strong and weak, and to hypothesize how it might be improved. Each technique gives different outputs, helping to create a more complete understanding:

- Which elements of the ad are emotionally engaging? (EEG, SST, biometrics or FAC)

- When does it grab attention? (EEG or SST)

- Does it have moments that are likely to be memorable? (EEG or SST)

- Of the most important concepts it's meant to evoke, which are succeeding and which aren't? (Implicit response)

It is one thing to convince a viewer to watch your ad (rather than fast-forward, switch channels or look away) and to engage with it; it is another to actually get them to engage with it to the point where they want to share it with their friends and family. Thales Teixeira, an assistant professor of marketing at Harvard Business School, has studied what makes online ads viral.[1] Creating a viral ad has multiple benefits: not only does it indicate that the ad is itself highly engaging, but its chances of being seen by many more people increase. Some ads succeed at this, achieving millions of views on video sites such as YouTube, thanks to people sharing the ad with their friends or on social networks. Such ads that have succeeded in this way in recent years include the Volkswagen ad featuring a young child dressed as Darth Vader from *Star Wars*, unsuccessfully attempting to make household objects move using 'the force', until his father makes the car start for him using a remote control. At the time of writing, this ad – called 'the force' – has been viewed over 61 million times on YouTube.

Teixeira and his colleagues conducted experiments with people watching ads online whilst being tracked using eye-trackers and automated facial coding. Whilst watching the videos they could choose to click away on to another video at any time. They found that adding surprise is an effective way of both grabbing and retaining viewers. Repeated moments of joy were also an effective component in retaining attention (although it may be worth bearing in mind that as there are only three positive emotions within the standard facial coding measurement repertoire, it might not be so surprising that two of them at least would show an increase during the best ads). They then followed up with an experiment in which the viewers could forward any video to their friends. Perhaps unsurprisingly, the main reason for sharing the videos was more interpersonal and social than it was driven by the bottom-up features of the video itself. Viewers simply wanted to look good in the eyes of friends or family by sharing the video. Examples of this type of ad include those that the viewer has had exclusive or preview access to, those that dramatize an individual's personal values in an interesting way, or that are unconventionally entertaining.

A final ingredient found by Teixeira and his team is something they call 'brand pulsing'. Showing a brand too prominently can provoke viewers to switch away, whereas not showing it enough can result in a lack of memory for the brand that created the ad. The brand-pulsing solution involves showing the brand regularly, but in an unobtrusive and brief way.

A third pattern for understanding the structure of a TV ad comes from SST (see Chapter 10), the technique for measuring real-time electrical brain activity. SST is particularly good at measuring long-term memory encoding. Whilst there are patterns that predict good emotional engagement and attention for an ad, there is also a structural pattern to ads that affects how likely we are to remember the branding.

As people watch an ad, their brain stores key moments of the narrative as 'snapshots', then, when they believe the ad to be finished, they will consolidate this series of snapshots into one memory for long-term storage. This process of consolidation takes around one to three seconds, during which any new information that appears is likely to be missed and hence not stored in memory. The process is analogous to a comedian pausing after they have just told a joke – they need to leave a few seconds for people to process it, before they can tell another one, or it will just be missed. With most ads placing the branding information at the very end, there is obviously the potential for this to be missed and not enter into long-term memory.

So what can be learned from these insights? Whilst every ad is different, and successful ads can work in different ways, there are a few things that these neuro measures would predict should work best. The need to grab attention early and to sustain it through the ad may be somewhat obvious; although perhaps the use of negative emotions to create tension may be less so. However, perhaps the key structural change to ads suggested from the neuro methods is the notion of brand pulsing. We also know from eye-tracking data that too much exposure to the brand logo can cause viewers to change channels. Showing the brand little and often may be a good way to maximize memory whilst minimizing people shifting their attention elsewhere.

Combining vendors

One of the most challenging ways of combining data can be to compare the results of studies from one vendor with that of another. The industry is still largely fragmented, particularly in EEG measures, in its definitions of measures or their interpretation. What one vendor means by 'engagement' will be different from another. Some vendors place most importance on memory, others on attention or emotion. Different vendors also have different experimental paradigms: they are structuring their tests differently, hence their data may not be immediately combinable. The raw data from eye-tracking, implicit response or biometrics may seem combinable, but even here there can be differences in experimental protocols that make it problematic. Also, differences in the recording equipment can make data hard to combine. For this reason, often the most useful databases are those comprised of exactly the same experimental designs, with the same type of media.

Combining with sales data

There is obviously a desire amongst clients to see hard data on correlations between research results and sales data. If the neuro methods say that an ad or package design is more effective, is this also demonstrably resulting in higher sales? As with any type of marketing research, pinning down such connections can be time-consuming, difficult and expensive. Myriad factors can influence sales data, including the general economic trends at the time, the activities of competitive brands and even the weather. Filtering out the effects of these real-world influences makes such exercises difficult and costly.

Equally, the funding for searching for these correlations has so far been minimal. There are no industry-wide bodies with the financial means to fund this type of research. The individual suppliers have historically mainly been reluctant to openly publish their methods and algorithms, potentially ceding their commercial advantage. Nevertheless, there have been successful yet unpublished exercises in correlating neuro measures with real-world commercial success. As the industry matures I expect more of these exercises to be published openly, and more organizations and companies to work together to form open standards for measurement.

Checklist

Comissioning and combining vendors

If you need to decide whether to commission one or multiple vendors for your research project, here are some things to consider:

☐ Make a list of the questions you need to answer with your research. Ask vendors what their techniques are best at measuring and compare this to your list. Beware of vendors who claim they have one technique that is good at answering every question (it is possible, however, that they may use multiple techniques).

☐ Ask the vendors to provide definitions for each of their metrics. For example, what do they mean exactly by 'engagement'?

☐ Consider whether you have more than one metric that you expect to be measuring the exact same thing (eg there are multiple methods for measuring emotional arousal). Is this surplus to your needs, or is this a good way for you to validate or at least compare different ways of measuring the same thing?

☐ Ask to see examples of materials that scored well and those that scored poorly on this metric.

☐ Ask to see a 'dummy' report that will enable you to see the format of the outputs you will get. Be clear about whether the measures are giving moment-by-moment or summarized results.

☐ Ask how many previous studies the vendor has done of the type that you need. How large is their database of previous similar studies?

☐ If you think you will need to combine measures from different vendors, ask them about their technical capabilities in doing so. For example, it is rare that two different vendors offering lab-based measures would combine measures, but they might with online measures. If the combination of measures is in parallel it might be as simple as one vendor conducting their measure, then providing a hyperlink over to the test of the second vendor. This kind of arrangement saves money by allowing you to use the same participants for both tests.

Summary

- Research methods all have their own strengths and weaknesses. By combining methods you can attain a bigger array of results, which can be more insightful.

- Some methods combine simultaneously, both giving moment-by-moment comparative scores. Others can be combined by one giving moment-by-moment scores and the other giving overall scores. A third way of combining methods is to run parallel studies on different yet related stimuli.

- Combining ostensibly the same metrics from different vendors is usually difficult, due to different definitions and different methods of measuring the same things.

Note

1 Nobel, C (2013) [accessed 24 April 2015] Advertising Symbiosis: The Key to Viral Videos, *Harvard Business School* [Online] http://hbswk.hbs.edu/item/7267.html.

CONCLUSIONS

14

In this book we have looked at a number of the theories and ideas that underpin how marketers, ad creators, designers and neuroscientists are using neuromarketing data. These ideas can both help in forming hypotheses for testing, and also in making sense of study results. We have seen how consumers' choices are swayed by non-conscious processes such as the ease with which we process information, the biases we have about value, and the fact that we can have associations and even goals activated in our minds without conscious awareness.

The field is still young, but a number of techniques have taken their place as regular methods in use daily around the world. Table 14.1 summarizes the main characteristics of each method: the examples of questions that each is good at answering, whether they can give moment-by-moment results (eg through the course of an ad) and whether they can be used online.

TABLE 14.1   Key features of the main neuromarketing methods

Method	Example Strengths	Moment by Moment?	Online?
Eye-tracking	Understanding whether a package 'pops out' on-shelf. Which positions of ads in a publication or web page are most likely to get viewed?	✓	✓
Implicit response	Measuring the comparative qualities that people associate with a brand and its competitors. Measuring the ability of an ad to communicate the messages, feelings and concepts it was intended to.	✓	✓
Facial coding	If an ad is intended to evoke one of the facial coding emotions (eg happiness or surprise) how well does it do so, at which moments, and how well in comparison to alternative edits or versions?	✓	✓
Biometrics	Measuring the ability of an ad or experience to create strong levels of emotional arousal.	✓	
fMRI	Understanding the overall performance of an ad, the specific feelings and reactions it produces, and predicting its likely marketplace performance.		
EEG	Measuring the flow of viewer attention through an ad, or the cognitive load of an experience or task.	✓	
SST	Understanding the elements of an ad that are likely to be best remembered.	✓	

The future

The field will almost certainly continue to grow in the future in both use and sophistication. Costs are coming down, and awareness of these techniques is increasing. I believe there will be three key trends in the years ahead: more validation; more understanding and insights; and new measures.

More validation

It can be a difficult and expensive exercise, but pressure from clients will drive more research into testing these metrics against real-world sales data. This will help provide a stronger rationale for use, as well as probably understanding more about how each method is best deployed.

More understanding and insights

Through more use, a greater understanding will likely accumulate about how and why different features in ads and communications perform well or poorly. Also the ever-increasing understanding of the brain, and understanding of how brain activity relates to real-world behaviours, will benefit the industry. As neuromarketing is very much a hybrid discipline, greater communication and understanding will develop between its component areas of specialism (eg neuroscience, marketing, design, usability, signal processing).

New measures

More metrics using current techniques will likely be developed, as well as more sophisticated and user-friendly outputs. One trend is towards online dashboards that allow clients to both set up studies themselves and then view the results with minimal help from the vendor.

There may even be new technologies available in the years ahead, such as increasingly sophisticated computational neuroscience tools, methods for coding behaviour from cameras, and cheaper and more user-friendly versions of fMRI recording. A new technology, still in its infancy, fNIRS (functional near infrared spectroscopy) may eventually take its place amongst the current neuromarketing tools. Looking similar to an EEG cap it measures blood flow in the brain (like fMRI) by shining near infrared light into the brain (this portion of the light spectrum is able to shine through the skin, tissue and bone of the scalp) and then detect the changes in the light due to blood flow at various positions in the brain.

Also there are a growing number of devices that consumers themselves own that can be used for tracking responses to commercial messages.

Wearable devices originally developed to track fitness parameters such as heart activity and movement could in theory be used, for example, to monitor the wearer's reactions to YouTube videos, where they shop and what they view online. The sensors in smartphones, combined with our use of them to access information online, and the fact that we carry them with us all the time means that they are potential conduits for monitoring consumer reactions too. Microsoft's current Xbox device has cameras capable of monitoring the heart rate (through subtle changes in skin colouration), emotional state (through facial analysis) and in which direction someone is looking. It can do this for up to six people at once, in their own living rooms. As the Xbox is sitting under the TV in millions of homes around the world the potential for using it to track responses to media is huge, but equally huge are the privacy and ethical concerns and potential consumer resistance. Such developments also hint at the possibility that whilst currently the neuromarketing industry is dominated by the large market research companies and a range of smaller specialists, in the near future the web and tech companies themselves, through their direct access to consumer and viewer responses, could become a more dominant player.

Limitations and ethical issues

There have always been ethical concerns raised by commentators about neuromarketing. This is perhaps natural, as a technology and body of knowledge (neuroscience) that had previously been pursued either for pure knowledge or for medical benefits was now being combined with raw commerce. The narrative of many media stories on the subject has essentially been: advertisers are homing in on your brain's buy button, and when they find it they will begin pressing it incessantly!

Most of the worries are not really unique to neuromarketing or are based on a misunderstanding of what neuromarketing can actually do. For example, all good researchers should adhere to the same, if not stricter, data privacy procedures as traditional market research, and concerns over marketing to children or marketing unethical or harmful products are not unique to this field. Equally, whilst it is difficult to judge, it seems that a majority of neuromarketing projects are ranking materials produced by creatives, ad producers and designers. In other words, the tests describe when the creatives get it right, but the power to produce the material is still in the hands of those creatives (albeit with some insights from neuro-science). Understanding consumers' thinking and emotions is complex, and there is no single buy button in the brain. Even if certain regions in the brain are associated with emotional or attentional engagement, or attraction or longing for a product, this does not give a direct mechanism for activating the interest and desires of consumers – that power is down to the work and creativity of product and ad creators. All neuromarketing researchers can currently do is help to hone these messages.

The overarching message of consumer neuroscience so far has perhaps been to advocate simplicity of design. Yet this is not a revolutionary idea, it was already an old trend when neuromarketing came along. Whether it is the clean lines of the font Helvetica, the Teutonic austerity of Braun's electronics goods, or the seductive simplicity of Apple's devices there has long been a trend over the last century towards a minimalist, form-as-function in design.

Nevertheless, as neuromarketing grows in power and reach it would be wise for independent observers to keep a watchful eye against intrusions of privacy and potential abuses of power that deep insights into consumers' non-conscious could provide.

Narrow explanations could become locked in

Whilst many commentators are worried that neuromarketing will become so good that it will be problematic, an unaddressed possibility is the opposite: the danger of it making incorrect assumptions about human responses.

There is an old joke about a drunk man spotted looking at the ground underneath a street light at night. When asked what he's doing he replies he's looking for his keys that he has lost. When then asked if he dropped them underneath the street light, he replies 'No, but this is the only place where the light is good enough to look!' Similarly, neuromarketing meas-ures could result in all the attention being focused on those things that we can measure, and the resulting models may forget those aspects of human experience that are not so amenable to measurement using these techniques. It is impossible to produce a list of what these might be as we don't yet know how far these measures might mine consumer reactions. However, a useful analogy might be psychology itself. Whilst cognitive neuroscience has been in the ascent, there are other schools of psychological research such as social psychology and the phenomeno-logical schools; the former considering the social context of human behaviour, the latter the lived conscious experience of people. Human tastes and fascinations evolve over time, in synch with the social context of the time, and whilst numerical data can give us many insights into a person's reactions, they can still never tell us exactly what it is like to be that person, with all their complex ways of experiencing and making sense of the world. If neuromarketing thinking becomes dominant, it may be important to keep these alternative sources of insight as a counterweight.

Doesn't measure longer-term reactions

The methods in this book mostly measure the short-term reactions to ads. However, this does not always capture people's full response. For example, the ending of an ad can change the meaning of the beginning when we think back, just as the end punchline changes our retrospective under-standing of the beginning of a joke. Yet jokes work as one-offs; ads typically need to work both as one-offs and repetitively. Some methods may capture a little of this changing type of reaction by showing the same ad repeatedly, but for economic and practical reasons this repetition is usually done in swift succession within the same session, and rarely over the course of days or weeks.

In this sense, the evaluation of consumer neuroscience to ad creative is the opposite of the gestalt school of film criticism, which appraises a film on whether as a whole it transcends the sum of its parts. You may have had the experience of watching a film that seemed nothing special at the time, yet in the days, months and years afterwards it lingers with you, having wormed its way into your non-conscious mind. The digestion of a piece of video or an image can rearrange our initial reactions, just as digesting a meal can leave us feeling anywhere from satisfied to sick.

Such limitations need to be borne in mind when evaluating the potential of neuromarketing methods. Equally, an ethical approach to using these methods should be adopted: if consumers feel overly manipulated, the backlash against your brand could be more harmful than the upside of learning from neuromarketing insights.

GLOSSARY

anchoring   The tendency for people's choices to be influenced (non-consciously primed) by preceding information, even if it has no rational relationship to the decision.

attentional blink   Brief moments of blindness to – or unawareness of – stimuli. For example if a sequence of images are seen in succession, if one image appears too quickly (around 180–450 milliseconds) after another it may not be consciously seen.

behavioural economics   The application of cognitive neuroscience and psychological insights into decision-making to model or explain economic behaviour.

bottom-up (processing)   Processing of the lower levels of sensory stimuli before fully comparing with memories or expectations.

bounded rationality   The notion that people are limited in their ability to be rational, by practical constraints such as the limited range of information they are aware of or by their environment (sometimes referred to as ecological rationality).

choice architecture   The way that choices are structured or presented to people (differences in choice architecture often change the that way people choose).

choice blindness   The tendency for people not to be fully aware of their choices or, when termed 'change blindness', to be unaware of the differences between options.

cognitive bias   A mental rule or heuristic (usually non-conscious) that results in a biased or irrational judgement, perception or decision.

cognitive neuroscience   Combines cognitive psychology with neuroscience to understand the neurological basis of different thought processes.

cognitive psychology   The study of the mental processes behind human behaviour. Includes processes such as attention, memory, perception and language.

computational neuroscience   The use of computer models to understand and predict brain activity.

cortex   The top part of the brain, most recent in evolutionary terms.

EEG (electroencephalography)   Measures of electrical brain activity.

embodied cognition   The use of bodily sensations or metaphors as a source of thinking, perception or choice (often non-conscious).

endowment effect   The tendency of people to value things more once they own them.

event boundaries   In relation to an ad or experience, the points that people mentally note as being the end of one section of meaning or narrative.

eye-tracking   The use of eye-tracking systems to measure where people are looking. This can be mobile or fixed under a screen.

facial action coding   Classification of emotional facial expressions (can be done manually or automated by computer).

fMRI (functional magnetic resonance imaging)   Measuring which areas of a person's brain are active by measuring blood flow in the brain. It requires that the person lies within a special scanner.

heuristic   A mental shortcut rule that people use to process sensory information or make choices (usually non-conscious).

hyperbolic discounting   The tendency for people to prefer rewards in the immediate present rather than the future (even if the future reward is somewhat larger).

implicit response measures   Psychological tests (often reaction-speed based) that measure non-conscious associations.

loss aversion   The tendency for people to be more motivated by the prospect of loss than the opportunity of gain.

low-involvement processing   Sensory processing with low levels of conscious, motivated attention.

neuroaesthetics   Insights from neuroscience into why we find certain things attractive or beautiful.

neuroeconomics   Using insights from neuroscience to understand people's economic choices. In theory, this covers similar territory to behavioural economics but tends to use 'harder' data such as direct brain measures and computational models (whereas behavioural economics tends to use more behavioural and social psychological data).

neuromarketing   Broadly: the use of brain and physiological measures – and insights from these to inform marketing decisions.

neuro-sales predictions   Using neuromarketing data to predict sales volumes. Currently this field is in its infancy.

non-conscious   The operations of the brain for which we do not have conscious awareness.

peak–end rule The tendency, when remembering an experience, to evaluate its emotional quality with disproportionate reference to the most intense moment and the end moment.

prediction markets Predicting the outcome of something (such as the likely box-office success of a movie) based on the average predictions of large numbers of people.

priming Exposure to something that then affects subsequent responses by activating non-conscious memory associations.

processing fluency The difficulty of mentally processing an idea or stimulus.

social proof The tendency for people to become biased in their choices by their perception of how others have chosen.

SST (steady state topography) Similar to EEG this is a measure of electrical brain activity, but it sets up a 'marker' frequency in the person's brain using a flickering light. As exposure to stimuli then makes the brain work, there are deviations in this frequency that allow us to see how hard areas of the brain are working.

subliminal The presentation of a stimulus or the processing of a stimulus of which we are not consciously aware.

supraliminal A stimulus that we can consciously perceive (but may choose to not pay attention to).

system 1 The fast, automatic and effortless processing of our non-conscious mind.

system 2 The effortful, slow (in comparison to system 1) and calculating processing of our conscious mind.

top-down (processing) Processing of sensory information based on memory and expectations.

working memory Our (limited) mental capacity for holding multiple bits of information in mind for considering or comparing them. Often used synonymously with 'short-term memory'.

Zeigarnik effect The tendency for people to remember unfinished or unresolved events more than those that are resolved.

FURTHER READING

Altman, M (2012) *Behavioral Economics for Dummies*, John Wiley & Sons, Ontario

Ariely, D (2009) *Predictably Irrational: The hidden forces that shape our decisions*, HarperCollins, London

Banaji, MR and Greenwald, AG (2013) *Blind Spot: Hidden biases of good people*, Delacorte Press, New York

Barden, P (2013) *Decoded: The science behind why we buy*, John Wiley & Sons, London

Claxton, G (1994) *Noises from the Darkroom: The science and mystery of the mind*, Aquarian, London

Claxton, G (1997) *Hare Brain Tortoise Mind: Why intelligence increases when you think less*, Fourth Estate, London

Dooley, R (2012) *Brainfluence: 100 ways to persuade and convince consumers with neuromarketing*, John Wiley & Sons, London

Ekman, P (ed) (2013) *Emotion in the Human Face*, 2nd edn, Malor, Los Altos, CA

Frijda, NH (2007) *The Laws of Emotion*, Routledge, London

Gawronski, B and Payne, BK (ed) (2010) *Handbook of Implicit Social Cognition*, The Guildford Press, London

Genco, SJ *et al* (2013) *Neuromarketing for Dummies*, John Wiley & Sons, Ontario

Gigerenzer, G (2007) *Gut Feelings*, Allen Lane, London

Gladwell, M (2005) *Blink: The power of thinking without thinking*, Penguin, London

Haugtvedt, CP, Herr, PM and Kardes, FR (eds) (2008) *Handbook of Consumer Psychology*, Psychology Press, New York

Heath, R (2012) *Seducing the Subconscious: The psychology of emotional influence in advertising*, Wiley-Blackwell, Oxford

Horsley, M *et al* (eds) (2014) *Current Trends in Eye Tracking Research*, Springer, London

Kahneman, D (2011) *Thinking, Fast and Slow*, Penguin, London

Lang, A (2011) (ed) *Measuring Psychological Responses to Media Messages*, Routledge, London

Lewis, D (2013) *The Brain Sell: When science meets shopping*, Nicolas Brealey, London

Lindstrom, M (2005) *Brand Sense: Sensory secrets behind the stuff we buy*, Kogan Page, London

Lindstrom, M (2008) *Buy.ology: How everything we believe about why we buy is wrong*, Random House, London

Martin, SJ, Goldstein, NJ and Cialdini, RB (2014) *The Small Big: Small changes that spark big influence*, Profile Books, London

Parasuraman, R and Rizzo, M (eds) (2008) *Neuroergonomics: The brain at work*, Oxford University Press, New York

Piattelli-Palmarini, M (1994) *Inevitable Illusions: How mistakes of reason rule our minds*, John Wiley & Sons, New York

Potter, RF and Bolls, PD (2012) *Psychophysiological Measurement and Meaning: Cognitive and emotional processing of media*, Routledge, London

Ramsøy, TZ (2014) *Introduction to Neuromarketing & Consumer Neuroscience*, Neurons Inc, Copenhagen

Rudman, LA (2011) *Implicit Measures for Social and Personality Psychology*, Sage, London

Sharp, B (2010) *How Brands Grow: What marketers don't know*, Oxford University Press, Melbourne

Sutherland, S (1992) *Irrationality*, Pinter & Martin, London

Thaler, RH and Sunstein, CR (2009) *Nudge: Improving decisions about health, wealth and happiness*, Penguin, London

Wilson, TD (2002) *Strangers to Ourselves: Discovering the adaptive unconscious*, Harvard University Press, London

Wittenbrink, B and Schwarz, N (eds) (2007) *Implicit Measures of Attitudes*, The Guildford Press, New York

INDEX

Note: The index is filed in alphabetical, word-by-word order. Numbers and acronyms within main headings are filed as spelt out. Page locators in *italics* denote information contained within a Figure or Table.

CPSIA information can be obtained at www.ICGtesting.com
Printed in the USA
BVOW06s1055140716

455565BV00006B/7/P